Class acts: stories from Emily Grif
374.978 Bri

P9-EJI-081

Silver City Public Library

Cl

DATE DUE

	SEP 3 0 2015		

Emily Griff

Class Acts

Stories from
Emily Griffith Opportunity School

Carolyn Brink

Foreword by
Denver Mayor John W. Hickenlooper

SILVER CITY PUBLIC LIBRARY
515 W. COLLEGE AVE.
SILVER CITY, NM 88061

374.978
Bri

0248189
$13   1/11

This book is dedicated to the memory of
two special women, Emily Griffith
and my mother, Helen Brink

ISBN-13: 978-0-86541-079-4
ISBN-10: 0-86541-079-8
Library of Congress Control Number: 2006928903

Copyright © 2006 Carolyn Brink
ALL RIGHTS RESERVED

Photographs of story subjects by Carolyn Brink, with the exception of Flora Gasser, Gabriela
Bowman, and Elizabeth Cohill who supplied their own photos. Photograph of Myrle K. Wise
courtesy Denver Fire Department. Historic photos are courtesy of Emily Griffith Opportunity
School.

Published by
Filter Press, LLC
P.O. Box 95
Palmer Lake, CO 80133

No part of this book may be mechanically or electronically reproduced without written
permission of the publisher. For information contact Filter Press 719-481-2420 or email to
info@filterpressbooks.com.

Manufactured in the United States of America.

For more information about the Emily Griffith Opportunity School, contact the
Emily Griffith Foundation at 720-423-4722, or at www.egos-school.com/egf.

Contents

Foreword

Emily Griffith shines in Denver's history book. Spunky, compassionate, and driven, Griffith was a little lady with a big idea: to open a school for adults. Much more than a woman with a unique idea, Emily Griffith was a Denver power broker who knew how to work with the community and Denver Public Schools to see her brainchild come to fruition.

The Emily Griffith Opportunity School has operated continuously for nearly ninety years in its same downtown Denver location and is now a beloved local institution with a worldwide reputation. Diverse groups of people congregate under the school's welcoming roof. The wealthy rub elbows with the poor, the old with the young, English-speaking with non-English-speaking. During a particularly inspiring visit with fifty-two students at the school, I was amazed to learn that thirty-six languages were spoken among them.

Since opening its doors in 1916, the school has served nearly 1.5 million people. That's close to three times the population of the city and county of Denver. There are few square blocks in the Mile High City that have positively impacted as many lives as the square block at 13th and Welton streets.

While Emily Griffith and her school have a rich and fascinating history, the stories of students who have walked through its doors are equally captivating.

The first of its kind, *Class Acts: Stories from Emily Griffith Opportunity School* weaves together the history of the school with narratives of selected alumni. For these individuals, their journeys with the Emily Griffith Opportunity School were life-changing experiences, which in turn, have had a ripple effect, benefiting countless others.

Through her interviews with alumni of the Emily Griffith Opportunity School, author Carolyn Brink captures the impact of the life of a selfless woman who chose to leave Denver—and the world—a better place than it was when she was born into it. In the true spirit of Emily Griffith herself, Carolyn—who was obviously touched by the school during her time as an administrator there—is donating the proceeds from this book to the Emily Griffith Opportunity School Foundation.

As systems of public education and higher education are increasingly scrutinized, *Class Acts* provides hope and demonstrates how a slight nudge from a nurturing educational institution can propel individuals, one person at a time, to more fulfilling lives.

Mayor John W. Hickenlooper
City and County of Denver

Preface

"Who knows what undiscovered greatness will be revealed in our pupils?" Emily Griffith asked her assistant this question as they exited Opportunity School at the conclusion of its first day of operation on September 9, 1916. Now, nine decades and 1.5 million students later, even Emily would be overwhelmed by the greatness uncovered in those who have attended her school.

The students at this world-renowned institution in downtown Denver, Colorado, have been as diverse as the city itself. In cashing in on Emily's dream of providing education "for all who wish to learn," many have made personal sacrifices, overcome tremendous odds, and gone on to contribute significantly to their communities.

I worked as an administrator at Emily Griffith Opportunity School (EGOS) from 1987 to 2002. I saw firsthand how many students made incredible personal sacrifices to find educational success—often for the first time. I decided to tell their stories.

Twenty-four former EGOS students shared their personal histories with me. Each tape-recorded face-to-face interview lasted approximately two hours. The resulting chronicles feature alumni who represent a broad cross-section of the whole. While the interviewed subjects were selected at random, I attempted to represent diverse program areas and cover a range of time periods of attendance.

Emily Griffith students are class acts. Many have overcome goose bump–raising odds. Their profiles are punctuated with human pain, courage, joy, and triumph. Testifying to the impact of the school in transforming lives and unleashing success, these student stories collectively demonstrate the uplifting effect of Emily's dream.

In commemoration of the school's ninetieth anniversary, I have written *Class Acts* to honor Emily Griffith Opportunity School and its inspiring students. Proceeds from this book will be donated to the Emily Griffith Foundation for student scholarships and programs.

– Carolyn Brink

Introduction

Emily Griffith
The Original Class Act

*"I already have a name for the school.
It is Opportunity."*

As a young girl, Emily Griffith experienced firsthand the brutality of poverty, yet in adulthood she left the comfort and security of a cushy state Department of Education job to teach at a school in the Denver slums. She promoted the virtues of good citizenship to her students but "fudged" on her age when she first arrived in the city.

Emily never had an enemy, but she was murdered in 1947, a case that remains unsolved to this day. These perplexing contradictions might imply Emily Griffith was a complicated woman. She was not.

Her deep compassion for people, particularly the down-and-out, unlocked the doors to adult education. From humble beginnings, Emily, a small, slender woman with expressive eyes, rose to become one of Colorado's most respected and influential citizens through her pioneering efforts as the founder of Opportunity School.

Emily was born in 1868 in Cincinnati, Ohio. Her father, Andrew, an attorney, barely scratched out an existence for his family that included his wife, Martha; son, Charles; and daughters Emily, Florence, and Ethelyn. Emily's mother appeared frail. Emily's father walked with a limp. And her sister Florence was considered simpleminded—the term applied to developmentally delayed people in the late nineteenth century.

Andrew Griffith refused to take on legal cases that he did not believe in. Consequently, the family struggled and moved often, and the children's education was sporadic at best.

In 1884, the family moved to central Nebraska to homestead on an unwelcoming, harsh prairie. They hoped to find financial success as landowners and planted their roots on 160 acres in the state's Arnold Precinct. Emily was sixteen. The new environment provided tough challenges for survival. The vicious weather tested their endurance. Frigid winters brought blinding blizzards, and scorching summers hosted drought, hailstorms, and ambushing tornadoes. But the biggest obstacles centered on making ends meet. When Emily was in her late teens, she stepped up to the plate to assist her family financially. It would launch a role she would assume for the rest of her life.

The rugged prairie offered few employment opportunities for young women. The most plentiful were in teaching, as young female teachers, upon marrying, relinquished their jobs. Although her education had gaps because of her family's frequent moves, Emily had been a good student and an avid reader. Confident in her skills, she applied for a teaching position and interviewed before a three-man school board. The all-male interviewing team appeared skeptical of their young, petite applicant. Emily's flashy blue eyes radiated a spark of self-assurance in spite of her lack of experience.

The board grilled her. After demonstrating her reading ability, she tested in spelling. Asked to spell *vicissitudes,* she hesitated slightly and then rolled out the appropriate letters in a soft, gentle voice. On the chalkboard, she calculated math problems related to bushels of grain. By this time, Emily had won the hearts of two of the men. The lone holdout pressured her to demonstrate her penmanship on the chalkboard. Unsatisfied with her *s*, this reluctant board member sparked spontaneous laughter from his colleagues and Emily with his reaction. Emily modified her *s*, and the board offered her a job teaching in a sod schoolhouse near Broken Bow in central Nebraska.

She lived with local rural families, rotating lodging between farms. The parents of her students were primarily Swedish, Norwegian, German, and Bohemian immigrants. Many did not know how to read, write, or calculate whether they had been paid fairly for their farm products, so Emily spent her evenings teaching the adults as well. Living in sod houses where the wind blew through the walls and fleas infested the straw-covered floors, Emily learned she could address the problems of her rural constituents through personal instruction. In these humble surroundings, Emily's idea for adult education germinated.

Teaching in a one-room schoolhouse where the ages and abilities of her students were varied and diverse challenged her. But Emily enjoyed her work, developed compassion for her students and their families, and discovered that teaching meant much more to her than just a means of contributing to her family's finances. It became her passion.

On the cruel Nebraska landscape, only the heartiest survived. The fragile Griffith clan did not. In 1895, Andrew Griffith packed up his family and headed west to Denver in hopes of finding fortune. In this new setting, Emily would once again be expected to contribute to the family coffers.

Moving to Denver brought new beginnings. Andrew Griffith became a missionary. Emily capitalized upon this new opportunity by "changing" her age. On the Denver schools employment records, she listed her year of birth as 1880, shedding twelve years. Although no one knows for sure why she chose to do this, many have speculated she did not want to admit to being twenty-seven, the age of "official spinsterhood," at that time. Ever after, Emily declined to list a year for her birthday and even snubbed the Who's Who award because it required her year of birth. Biographer Elinor Bluemel wrote: "Denver School records give the date as February 10, 1880 and Emily signed birthday books under the date of February 10, leaving out the year of her birth. 'I never tell my age,' she once said."[1]

Lacking qualifications for full teaching status in the Denver schools, Emily started as an alternate teacher at Central School. By 1896, she had gained enough experience to be assigned a regular position at this school, teaching in the sixth grade.

As it had in Nebraska, Emily's school day did not end with the final bell. Integrating insights gained near Broken Bow, she visited the homes of her students and witnessed much poverty, domestic abuse, and alcoholism. These home visits not only deepened her compassion for her students, they expanded her insights into why some found it difficult to learn and dropped out of school. Rather than being put off by the deplorable conditions, Emily was propelled to address them.

Emily acquired additional education, attending summer instruction at Denver Normal School. Over time, she amassed twenty-eight weeks of instruction and obtained a complimentary state teaching diploma. She remained at Central School until 1904, when she accepted the position of assistant state superintendent of public instruction. Except for a two-year break to return to teaching, she worked in this statewide position until 1912. The job introduced Emily to many people, marshaled her self-confidence, honed her persuasion skills, and provided important contacts for the future. Nonetheless, she preferred the classroom and direct contact with students.

Emily's path was never easy. As the primary breadwinner for her family, she sidestepped the offers of at least three suitors, one in Nebraska and two in Denver, to care for her family. One suitor,

Fordyce P. Cleaves, a young Denver teacher, had secured Emily's promise of marriage. Their relationship unraveled as Emily discovered similarities between her father and her husband-to-be. While both were eloquent, neither offered much promise as a provider. Emily had also assumed responsibility for her disabled sister, Florence, and Cleaves asked her to relinquish these duties upon their marriage. Emily refused. Years later, a Denver columnist wrote: "Cleaves told his sweetheart that he would not marry her unless the sister was sent away. The engagement was broken. If she had yielded, had rid herself of the burden, they no doubt would have married. But she spent her long life tending the helpless sister, putting her love and strength into her work as a teacher."[2] Cleaves dropped out of Emily's life. Later, an unnamed army officer also pursued Emily, but nothing came of this relationship.

In 1912, Emily accepted an eighth-grade teaching position at Twenty-fourth Street School at 24th and Walnut Streets. Located in an impoverished Denver neighborhood, the home conditions of her students mirrored those she had experienced in rural Nebraska. However, Emily thrived in this environment. Bluemel writes:

> The school was in a poor Denver neighborhood, many of her pupils were foreigners, there was much truancy and absence from school for other reasons. She began to look up the absent children outside of regular school hours. She found poverty and ignorance and crime. She spent much of her salary trying to help out with the poverty; but soon she realized this was not the solution.[3]

She ran her own night classes at the Twenty-fourth Street School for the uneducated adults in that neighborhood. Later, she taught district-sponsored evening classes at Longfellow School and Manual High School. Like her father the missionary, Emily developed an evangelistic zeal to improve lives. She set her sights on helping the down-and-out. The solution would be education, and Emily aimed to start such a school for this population.

Using skills she had acquired at her state job, Emily "worked" the community. Her warm personality, passionate conviction, and shameless advocacy for others swayed people to support her idea, revolutionary as it was. She enthusiastically shared her unique vision with anyone who would listen. This included not only her friends but also school, business, and community leaders. In December 1915, Emily brought her students and their families to the *Denver Post* clothing drive, where donated clothing was distributed to the needy. There Emily encountered Frances "Pinky" Wayne, an influential *Post* writer. She seized the opportunity to "bend" Wayne's ear:

> I wonder if you will let me tell you of a hope I have for the people in and out of my school, the boys and girls, their parents, too, whose education has been limited? I want the age for admission lifted and the classes so organized that a boy or girl working in a bakery, store, laundry, or any kind of shop, who has an hour or two to spare, may come to my school and study what he or she wants to learn to make life more useful. The same goes for older folks, too. I know I will be laughed at, but what of it? I already have a name for the school. It is Opportunity.[4]

Fascinated, Wayne helped Emily champion her cause. According to author Debra Faulkner, in *Touching Tomorrow*, her 2006 biography of Griffith, Wayne helped persuade many influential Denver citizens, including her newspaper bosses, Frederick Bonfils and Harry Tammen, to support the idea. Emily's concept gained momentum. Denver buzzed with the possibility of an opportunity school. Through Emily's persistence, public relations, and political skills, the Denver Schools agreed to give it a try. In 1916, Emily's dream unfolded.

The school district assigned Emily the condemned Longfellow School. Formerly an elementary school, it was an old, rundown two-story brick building at 13th and Welton streets in downtown Denver. Dark and dingy, the building contained many walls with dangling, ragged wallpaper and exposed surfaces with no paint. The district allocated her five devoted teacher assistants. Because no provisions had been made for preparing the building, Emily and her new staff scoured the facility over the summer in preparation for its fall opening.

Emily was fueled by the school district's confidence. Her annual salary of $1,800, which included day and evening work, was meager.

While the school district gambled on Emily's idea, not everyone eagerly embraced her concept. Some in the educational establishment regarded the proposed school with skepticism. Emily's success eventually silenced her critics. On September 9, 1916, the doors to Opportunity School opened. Outside the door, a large sign stated, PUBLIC OPPORTUNITY SCHOOL. Underneath it read, FOR THOSE WHO WISH TO LEARN. Emily had borrowed this slogan from her Uncle Charles, who ran a boat along the Erie Canal. Self-educated, Charles docked his vessel at night and hung a lantern to light a sign that contained this same phrase. He invited uneducated river workers aboard to learn. Like her uncle, Emily was intent on illuminating the minds and improving the lives of those who had been kept out of the traditional modes of learning.

While Emily had advertised the school's opening, she worried that no students would enroll. At best, she hoped to teach 200 in the first year. Preparing for the first day, she positioned her rolltop desk at the top of the stairs in the main entry, where it stayed the remainder of her tenure at the school. She personally greeted and assisted each student. To her delight, more than 1,400 eager learners walked through the doors the first week. Nearly 2,400 enrolled the first year. Their education was free, with the school district providing meager supplies.

Opportunity's doors were open from 8:30 a.m. to 9:30 p.m. Emily's school was an instant success. It welcomed immigrants eager to take English classes and to become citizens. Emily listened to what each student wanted and provided that instruction, even if it meant scrambling to find the right teachers. If a young man walked into her school and wanted to learn to make signs for his job, she provided the training. If no one on staff had the knowledge to teach this skill, she hired someone from the business world. Emily's unwavering commitment to a welcoming, friendly atmosphere also fueled the school's impressive triumph. This was a natural extension of Emily's personality. In fact, she threatened to fire teachers who refused to be cheerful. At one of her infrequent teachers' meetings, Emily said: "No one in our school is supposed to frown. Any one of the staff who is heard to speak a harsh word is subject to immediate dismissal."[5]

A photograph taken in the 1920s depicts Emily pointing to a chalkboard on which is posted the phrase, HELP ONE ANOTHER. This charitable philosophy infiltrated the school. Emily practiced what

Emily (third from right) encouraged students and staff.

she preached. Many attending night classes fainted from hunger as a result of dashing to school directly from work. To remedy this, Emily and her sister Florence stocked a large, steaming kettle of hot soup to feed the hungry pupils. From her salary, Emily also loaded her pockets with nickels, discreetly handing needy students the coins required for their streetcar fare home.

Introduction

Opportunity School passed its two-year trial period and flourished. Through the years, it continued to grow and expand. Knowing adults needed to plan their school schedules around work and family, Emily designed the coursework so students could begin when they wanted and exit when they had acquired the skills they needed. Courses were added and deleted, depending on student and labor market demands. Classes focused on basic skills, vocational training, and English language acquisition skills.

Under Emily's leadership, the school became the pride of the Mile High City. By 1933, more than 100,000 students had walked through Opportunity's doors. Word spread about this successful, innovative school. Visitors from around the globe flocked to its doors. Many other cities and countries, including France, Russia, Germany, and Great Britain, tried to lure Emily away to start similar schools. She was not tempted. The school at 13th and Welton streets was her home away from home, her life, and her passion. She belonged there like chalk on a blackboard. For seventeen years, from 1916 to 1933, Emily devoted her life to her school. By 1933, she felt she had accomplished her mission, and she decided to retire. Based on her age in the school's records, she was exiting early. However, her actual age was sixty-five; she was retiring on target.

Retirement brought changes to both Emily and the school. In 1934, a few months after her departure, the district changed the institution's official name to Emily Griffith Opportunity School. Initially, Emily resisted this. Friends convinced her it was only a matter of time before some official's name would be attached to the school, and Emily's was the only one deserving this honor. Reluctantly, she acquiesced.

Once she turned the reins of the school over to others, Emily felt she needed to physically distance herself from the building. She and Florence moved to Pinecliffe, Colorado, a small, sleepy mountain community near Boulder. Subsisting on Emily's paltry $50 per month retirement—a sum Emily requested because it was equal to what her teachers received in their pensions—the women lived simply in a primitive cabin. Still, her life was full. Emily's warm personality attracted new friends. On Sundays, she taught Bible classes in her home, and whenever she wanted fellow villagers to stop for a chat, she banged the washtub outside her door. Friends from Denver often journeyed to see her, and she occasionally returned to the city, primarily to give a speech or accept an award.

Over the years, Emily received a multitude of awards including Woman of the Year in 1927 from the Business and Professional Women of Denver, Inc.; honorary recognition from the Kiwanis; the Eminent Service Award from the Colorado Press Association; and several honorary degrees from state colleges and universities. Nominated by the *Denver Post,* Emily received Denver car license Number 1 in 1932 for her selfless contributions to education and humanity.

Perhaps Emily's greatest honors came posthumously. In 1954, the city dedicated a memorial fountain to Emily Griffith in the Civic Center. In 1975, the state of Colorado enshrined her picture in stained glass at its capitol, and in 1986, when the window was relocated within the statehouse, the governor signed an executive order honoring Emily and proclaiming February 10, 1986, as her 106th birthday. With this proclamation, the myth of Emily's 1880 birth year became officially set in stone. Other honors included the Colorado Business Hall of Fame selecting her for induction in 1996 and the mayor's Millennium Award in 2000 as one of fourteen dynamic individuals whose positive impact continues to benefit Denver.

As her life brought forth headlines, so did her death. Her unpredictable end shocked everyone. On June 19, 1947, she and her sister were found murdered in their cabin. Their plain wooden supper table had been set for three. Mashed potatoes, chili, and a pie waited on the stove. The cabin showed no signs of forced entry. Emily and her sister, each killed by a single gunshot wound, lay dead in their bedrooms, blood spattered on the walls. Two more unlikely murder victims could not have been found.

Suspicion soon focused on Fred Lundy, a former Opportunity School teacher, who lived near them and who had assisted them. Many believed he fostered romantic interests in Emily. Acquaintances reported he had been distressed over the primitive way in which the women lived. He had also become more agitated about Emily caring for her increasingly burdensome sister. A few weeks after the Griffith sisters' deaths, Lundy was found dead, assumed to be suicide. The case was never officially solved, although authorities believed they correctly identified Lundy as the murderer.

Emily died in 1947, but her legend lives on. An ordinary woman with an extraordinary idea, she pioneered a revolutionary school ninety years ago that remains at the same location in downtown Denver. Opportunity School continues to provide education for all who wish to learn. The school has left its mark on nearly 1.5 million people since 1916. Its continuous operation is a testament to its vitality, its importance in the community, and to Emily's vision. An even greater tribute to Emily's vision is the throng of alumni who made and continue to make significant contributions in their workplaces and communities. Ultimately, the legacy of this uncomplicated, yet profound, woman lives on through them.

Notes

1. Elinor Bluemel, *Emily Griffith and the Opportunity School of Denver* (Denver: Privately printed, 1954), 5.
2. Francis Plumb, "If She Had Married," *Rocky Mountain News,* June 18, 1954, 43.
3. Bluemel, *Emily Griffith and the Opportunity School,* 14.
4. Elinor Bluemel, *The Opportunity School and Emily Griffith, Its Founder* (Denver: Green Mountain Press, 1970), 9.
5. Bluemel, *Emily Griffith and the Opportunity School,* 36.

Emily Griffith, at right, with her long-time assistant, Mary Miller, and Paul Essert who followed Emily as principal of Opportunity School.

One
Surviving and Thriving
1916–1954

Opportunity School opened in 1916 in the Longfellow School at 13th and Welton in Denver. The building was razed in 1956.

Class Acts

Between 1916 and 1954, Emily Griffith Opportunity School (EGOS) catapulted from a far-fetched idea many doubted would work to a world-renowned institution. When the school opened in 1916, its philosophy of providing free adult education tailored to the unique needs of each individual student in a flexible, no-attendance-taking environment seemed like a recipe for failure. Instead, it proved to be a model for success. During this period, the school rode the waves of two world wars and a major depression, and its annual enrollment skyrocketed from 2,398 in 1916 to 29,570 in 1954.

Shortly after the school opened, World War I erupted, and Opportunity responded by emphasizing vocational training for soldiers and civilians. A newly constructed machine shop trained civilian workers to meet requests for war orders. When the war ended, the school established a high school department to address the needs of returning soldiers.

As the school grew, so did its course offerings. Classes for immigrants in English and citizenship swelled. By offering courses in hair weaving in 1917 and becoming the first public school in the country with courses in beauty training, Opportunity School was criticized for capitulating to "frills." However, Emily Griffith responded by saying, "The day will come when there will be a beauty parlor in every little town."[1]

Beauty training started at the school in 1917.

School officials established apprenticeship classes to address the growing need for more skilled workers. Between World Wars I and II, many craftsmen had immigrated to the United States to meet this demand. Government officials feared if American youth weren't trained by these craftsmen, the country would continue to rely on talent from overseas, thus displacing work for natives. National and state legislation passed and the school became a training center.

Emphasizing its vocational focus, the school established an employment bureau in 1928 to link workers with prospective employers. That same year, Opportunity School organized its own teachers' union, Local 203. Changes came forth in brick and mortar as well. The school constructed two additions to its Longfellow building, one in 1926 on 12th Street and another in 1947 between 12th and 13th streets on Welton Street. In 1951, the district built new shops on Glenarm Street.

During the Great Depression, thousands flocked to the school, hoping to obtain new skills to find work. In 1931, Opportunity's enrollment reached 9,500, with 1,000 prospective students on waiting lists because of the school's inadequate space and facilities. During this time, the school also offered courses to help financially strapped families stretch their limited resources. Students learned skills such as mending stockings and creating artificial floral arrangements.

In 1933, when the city was in the depths of the Depression, Emily Griffith retired as the school's principal. As its founder, she was the institution's heart and soul. Rumors circulated the school might close. However, the Denver Board of Education and the people of the city believed in Emily's vision and came to the rescue. To keep the school afloat, teachers accepted drastic salary cuts. The institution survived and even prospered during this precarious time. Rebounding from the depression in 1940, the school built an airframe shop, an auto shop, a mechanic shop, and a heat treatment plant, fortuitous additions that would benefit the defense efforts during World War II.

Additional changes occurred during World War II. More than fifty firms worked with EGOS to develop war-related courses such as shipbuilding, aero repair, pattern making, and heat treatment. The navy christened the school the "Shipyard of the Rockies" to symbolize its significant contributions to ship prefabrication. EGOS offered courses at Lowry Field. For a long period during the war, the school operated twenty-four hours a day, seven days a week, to train workers to support the military effort.

Attending school during World War II, a student is mastering skills in a nontraditional field.

In 1943, in an attempt to fill seats vacated by those serving in the military, Opportunity School invited Denver high school students to enroll in vocational training classes. The doors remained open to secondary students from that point forward. In spite of the war, new programs started, including restaurant training in 1942 and dental assisting in 1944. After the war, the school welcomed returning soldiers eager to capitalize on their veterans' benefits, obtain an

Opportunity School students supported the World War II effort.
In this July 1944 photo, EGOS students repair army vehicles.

Citizenship classes were popular during the school's early years.

education, and get on with their lives. The school also opened its doors to war refugees, primarily from Eastern Europe, yearning to leave behind devastating pasts.

In the postwar period, Opportunity continued to introduce new programs. In the 1950s, the school launched its practical nurse program. Its business education department expanded as well, to address the swelling need for office workers. The school accelerated its offerings in typing, shorthand, and bookkeeping. It launched courses in the insurance field and branched out into comptometer operations and keypunching. The Parent Education and Preschool Program, started in the city in 1927, came under the auspices of EGOS in 1953. Courses in distributive education, primarily preparing people for retail work, also took off in the 1950s.

Vocational courses have attracted and trained
students throughout the school's history.

With the school's budget plentiful, adults eager to learn, and the country in an optimistic postwar era, the school became all things to all people. EGOS introduced courses and lectures on public affairs, art appreciation, travel, and psychology. Many classes posted long waiting lists for entry.

The school matured from infancy to adulthood. Thousands of people of every color, age, and background tapped EGOS to uncover their potential and to prove Emily's words, "We do not believe in failure."[2]

The stories of seven disparate individuals, impacted by the effects of poverty, war, and hardship, but united by Emily's dream, follow in this section.

Notes

1. Elinor Bluemel, *Emily Griffith and the Opportunity School of Denver* (Denver: Privately printed, 1954), 48.
2. Elinor Bluemel, *The Golden Opportunity* (Boulder: Johnson Publishing Company, 1965), 17.

ISRAEL STUHL
Holocaust Survivor, Insurance Executive

"There were many people in the English classes, many from Eastern Europe. In accounting, I took a class with a Texan who had never met a Jew, and I had never met a Texan."

The dark blue tattooed numbers A6496 on Israel Stuhl's left forearm etch the history of his cruel, painful past. For Israel, this includes internment in four Nazi concentration camps, the death of his parents and five siblings in the Holocaust, and the devastating effects of tuberculosis.

Like many others, Israel's journey to Emily Griffith Opportunity School was arduous. He was born in 1929 in Slatinska Doly, Czechoslovakia. In 1944, he had completed the eighth grade when the Nazis invaded his country and collapsed any sense of security in his ghetto neighborhood. The Nazis captured the Jews, including Israel, his parents, and seven siblings, and marched them to the railroad station. There the Nazis loaded them onto cattle cars headed for the Auschwitz-Birkenau concentration camp. For three days, Israel and his family stayed on the crowded railcar, human waste piling up around them. They were given no water; their only food was what little they had brought from home.

Life in the Concentration Camps

At the concentration camp, they first encountered Joseph Mengele, the notorious Nazi doctor, who acquired the title "Angel of Death" because he sent countless Jews to their demise. He sorted people into two lines: those to be sent to the work camps and those who were going immediately to the gas chambers. "They separated the old people, the women, and the very young…These people were sent to the gas chambers. My mother and four younger siblings were killed immediately. Thousands of people were killed every day."

Slender with a receding hairline, a thick white moustache, and wire rim glasses, Israel recites his tortuous story from his beautiful brick home located on a quiet cul-de-sac in east Denver. He speaks in a soft, gentle voice with an accent. His tall, angular body slumps in deep concentration as he describes his heart-wrenching experiences of the Holocaust, a wholesale slaughtering of Jews between 1933 and 1945.

During his internment, Israel toiled at a factory that produced methanol and cyanide, which in addition to other uses were the gases piped into death chambers. "We worked from 6:00 a.m. to 6:00 at night. In the morning, all we got to eat was a piece of bread and coffee. At noontime, we broke for half an hour and we got soup. At 6:00, we came back from work and we got more soup. A lot of people died."

"People were 'selected' from working camps for the gas chambers. Selections were the worst part…If they thought you couldn't do the work, you were sent to the gas chamber. I was tall, just growing, fifteen years old, thin." Family and friends in the camp feared Israel wouldn't make the cut.

Israel seemed oblivious to being in jeopardy because he worked hard and produced every day. "I was lucky. They didn't select me."

Although he would escape the ultimate sentence, his life as a prisoner was brutal. From the first camp, the prisoners trudged to the Auschwitz-Buna, Buchenwald, and Theresienstadt concentration camps. "We marched from camps to train stations at night because they didn't want the German civilians to see what was going on. It was cold like Minnesota…We were shipped on open railcars, and many people froze to death. Without respect, the Germans threw bodies off the train."

The horrors continued. "At Buchenwald, we were in a sub-camp called the 'death camp' because people were dying. All we got to eat was a cup of coffee and a piece of bread once a day." Their thin weak bodies shivered in the cold. Yet the cold also minimized the stench of death that permeated their lives. "At the barracks every morning, they would take out dead bodies. They were dying in bunks all around me."

Under such horrific conditions, many would welcome death. Israel held on. "In the barracks in the one camp, there was an assistant barrack leader who was also Jewish. He would gather us together and try to give us hope. He told us we had to survive. When you hear that, you try your best."

Immigrating to the United States

Israel's family was separated. Members were sent to different camps. Israel struggled daily to stay alive. Finally, in the spring of 1945, the war ended in Europe. After more than a year in captivity, Israel, his two brothers, and his sister were reunited. They learned their father had been shot to death as he helped a young friend who had passed out while marching. Israel's sorrow deepened when, shortly after their liberation, his oldest brother died from a disease contracted in the camps.

The carefree days of youth were not to be for Israel. By 1945, at the age of sixteen, he had experienced a painful barrage of heartbreak, suffering, and grief. From that point forward, his life would be viewed through the Holocaust prism. In spite of his sorrowful past, his credo remained one of optimism and perseverance—to keep going and to keep trying.

Within months of his liberation, Israel and his siblings were relocated to a displaced person camp in Bavaria. "I knew I wanted to come to America. I had two aunts here, it was a big country: two oceans and no war." His brother and sister agreed the United States provided hope for a brighter future. They started learning English in the camp. Within four years, his brother and sister immigrated to the United States, eventually making their homes in Los Angeles.

Israel, however, would have to stay behind. He contracted tuberculosis, which delayed his departure. Highly contagious, TB spreads through the air from person to person and settles in the lungs or throat. Israel's weak immune system had made him susceptible.

In 1950, Israel had recovered enough to embark upon a journey to his new life in the United States. Jewish Family and Children's Services in Denver, Colorado, agreed to sponsor him. Going to Denver would be a bonus because the Mile High City provided one of the best climates in the United States for recovering TB patients.

However, Israel's road to a new life was not to be straight and smooth. The rough boat trip across the Atlantic caused a TB relapse. The jagged waves lashed against the ship, rocking and rolling Israel into a sick, weak shred of human life. For the first time in years, fresh tasty food was at his fingertips, but he could not partake of the fragrant, juicy oranges or crisp, red apples. The squelching summer heat compounded his discomfort. "I was so seasick," he said. "I lost fifteen pounds. The trip was eighteen days, and the sea was very rough." Nonetheless, with quiet dignity and inner strength, he forged ahead toward a better life, albeit penniless, sick, and with limited English.

Reduced to skin and bones, Israel arrived in Denver weary and weak. Immediately, he landed in the hospital at the Jewish Consumptive Relief Society on West Colfax, now the JCRS Shopping Center. The sterile hospital was his home for the next three years.

Attending Opportunity School

Within a year, his health had improved enough that he could leave the facility on a daily basis to attend classes at Emily Griffith Opportunity School. In 1951, nearly seven years after being sent to the camps, Israel was able to reclaim his life. Determined to transcend tragedy, he started taking English and accounting classes for four hours a day. "The teachers were very patient, especially with foreigners. My accounting classes were smaller, but more structured. We had to follow worksheets and a textbook. I really had a good experience there. Good memories. Going there was strictly for school. I was sick so I couldn't socialize since there was a stigma associated with TB." Recognizing others feared contracting the disease, Israel kept his distance. However, he developed special friendships with other TB survivors, a bond that, in many cases, has remained strong to this day.

"There were many people in the English classes, many from Eastern Europe. In accounting, I took a class with a Texan who had never met a Jew, and I had never met a Texan."

Fifty years later, at age seventy-five, Israel resurrects fond memories of the school that helped change his life. He recalls one English teacher's difficulty explaining the meaning of *modify*. Sensing she was making little headway, the instructor finally lifted her skirt and indicated she had modified the length of her garment.

Sitting in his kitchen, the refrigerator softly buzzing in the background, Israel holds a small black-and-white picture of his favorite English teacher. She sits behind a desk. On the blackboard behind her, "Merry Christmas" is written in several languages. While in the TB hospital many years earlier, Israel had tooled a leather billfold for one of his favorite teachers. His historical file reveals a warm thank-you letter from that instructor, written in perfect penmanship in blue fountain ink. Israel holds the letter's envelope, showing a 1953 postmark with a three-cent stamp. His hands, with long thin fingers, rest on the soft cream-colored cotton lace tablecloth.

Building a New Life

By 1953, he had completed two years at Emily Griffith. He was also released from the hospital. Immediately, he landed employment as a bookkeeper for National Farmers Union Insurance Companies, headquartered in Denver. "I was hired for $1.05 per hour. That was very acceptable then." An employment agency helped him secure the position, for which he paid the service one-half of his first month's salary.

His entry-level job stretched into a thirty-four-year career with the insurance company. Highly motivated, Israel accessed every educational and professional growth opportunity available. "Within the company, we were able to take additional insurance accounting courses. They were self-taught, independent study courses...I took quite a few...It was enjoyable. It taught me about things that I was doing. It helped me advance." The company routinely promoted him, eventually to an officer position as an assistant comptroller. He supervised a large staff, many with college degrees, and administered the division's accounting functions. And his only formal education came from Emily Griffith Opportunity School.

"If you want to succeed, you have to work hard. I worked long hours...and got the job done. I never blamed anyone if something went wrong. I said I was sorry, and I fixed it. I worked very hard. I got along with people...I was a fixture at that company," he says. His brown eyes dance as he pulls a sheet of paper from his work files that reflects his philosophy: "Lack of willpower and drive causes more failure than lack of intelligence and ability."

A good position with a stable company would not be the only sign that Israel had successfully made the transition to the United States. At the insistence of his older sister, who acted as his surrogate mother, he married at age thirty-six. "I didn't get married...because of the stigma of TB." He met his wife, Sari, a U.S. native, through his sister. Israel and his wife raised two sons who moved, as adults, to the Los Angeles area. Their sons each have two young boys, who are visited often by their Denver grandparents.

Israel's brother and sister, now deceased, remained in the Los Angeles area. Each married and had two children. Israel remains close to this extended family.

When asked about his philosophy of life, Israel says, "Life is to be kind to people, to be considerate of others. Gentleness and humility are enormous human strengths awaiting discovery by mankind."

As he walks in his manicured yard, shaded by mature trees exuding the fresh smells of spring, Israel shows compassion to his calico cat, Pebbles, who was in a fight the previous night. The cat's white, black, and tawny brown body appears battered and sore. With a gentle voice, Israel comforts her as she slithers through the patch of purple irises.

Having experienced a depth of pain few people know and having overcome incredible obstacles, Israel says, "I always believed that we can record the past, but we must live for the future."

<hr />

Author's Note: *I made three visits to Israel's home before completing the interview. Each time I saw him, my respect and admiration grew for this gentle, kind man. At the June 2002 graduation ceremonies, the Emily Griffith Foundation recognized him as the school's outstanding alumnus. Israel died in July 2005.*

MYRLE K. WISE
Denver's Top Fireman

*"I'm a real believer in Opportunity School...I consider
it one of the greatest institutions in the city of Denver."*

As a child, Myrle K. Wise often experienced the grimy, mushy taste
of dirt in his mouth. Born in 1918, he grew up in the 1930s
Dust Bowl of Oklahoma. His father participated in the "Sooner
Run" of the early 1900s, claiming four square miles of free acreage in the
state's panhandle, a desolate area so undesirable that the only way officials could attract settlers was to give away the land. With the promise
of an additional four square miles if he homesteaded and made improvements on the original acreage for at least five years, his father envisioned
a promising future. They raised wheat and cattle. And for a time, his dad

and mother and their family of seven children—three sisters older than Myrle and three brothers younger—survived.

Myrle's family valued education, and Myrle would eventually maximize his education from Emily Griffith Opportunity School to capture a high-ranking position. Emphasizing that each of their children must obtain a high school diploma, Myrle's parents sent their kids on horses to ride some five miles into the nearest town, Turpin, to attend high school.

Then the "Dirty Thirties" hit. Myrle remembers the wind ruthlessly swirling topsoil around their yard, making it impossible for them to see across their farm for months at a time. Often they would awaken in the morning to find one-quarter-inch-thick dust on the cloth of their dining table. Yet they persevered. Thanks to the chickens and cattle they raised, the family had food to eat. But little came forth from the soil.

From Dust Bowl to Denver

Between 1932 and 1936, Myrle attended high school. A star football and basketball player, he qualified for a college athletic scholarship. Tight family finances forbid such luxuries as college tuition. Other circumstances impeded their dream as well. By the time Myrle graduated from high school, his father had miraculously survived three bouts of dirt pneumonia. Few live through it once. Myrle's family knew if their father was to live, they needed to relocate. The day after Myrle's high school graduation in 1936, he took off with his dad to scout out a new future for the family. With relatives in Oregon, they headed west, toying with that as their end destination.

When they arrived in Denver, Myrle and his father thought they had discovered heaven. It was late spring, and as they pulled into the city, it was raining—the first moisture they had experienced in years. The green trees, fragrant flowers, and fresh atmosphere welcomed them better than any human could. Immediately, they knew they wanted to make this their home.

Myrle and his father found jobs with O. P. Bauers Candy and Ice Cream. Armed with a strong rural work ethic, both thrived at the company. At the end of the summer, the pair returned to Oklahoma to retrieve their family. Everyone relocated to Denver except one sister who stayed back with her husband to keep the family farm from being confiscated.

"We felt sorry for that sister, thinking we were leaving her there to starve," recalls eighty-six-year-old Myrle.

Ironically, years later that sister turned out to be the wealthiest of them all when oil was discovered on the land. The rest of the Wise siblings also prospered, enjoying success in such roles as bank president, construction company owner, and high-ranking policeman. Myrle became Denver's top fireman.

Studying and Teaching at Opportunity School

Sitting on the patio behind his brick home on busy Sheridan Boulevard, Myrle competes with traffic as his soft voice tells his story. Wind chimes, prompted by the gentle, warm summer breeze, jingle softly in the background. Tall and slender, with reddish hair and dark eyes, Myrle resembles a kind, gentle grandfather, but his words, enthusiasm, and memory reveal the youthful competence he displayed in his career as an effective city leader.

Myrle recalled the early years when he worked at the ice cream company seven days a week with a half day off on Sundays and Tuesdays. He made $7 weekly and was promoted to chief ice cream maker. Even with a steady income, finances were tight. In 1938, Myrle and his sweetheart, Evelyn, wanted to marry. She had just graduated from North High School, and they had hoped to wed on her birthday, July 10. However, Myrle's payday wasn't until July 12. Lacking the money for a marriage license, the couple delayed exchanging their vows until they had his paycheck in hand.

Although Bauers provided a steady income, Myrle itched for a more satisfying career. He dreamed of becoming a Denver fireman. However, at the end of the Depression, this was highly desirable work because it provided good pay, job security, and an opportunity for adventure. Hundreds applied for a handful of positions. Acceptance into the department was predicated on receiving a high score on the civil service test. Clever and motivated, Myrle was determined to qualify. He learned that Opportunity School offered a course to prepare for the test. The school's free tuition fit his budget, so he enrolled.

Attending Opportunity School for approximately six months and studying for his first civil service test, Myrle approached the exam with confidence. His photographic memory also helped. To his delight and relief, his score ranked in the top six out of more than 1,200 men who tested. He was also the only one of the six high qualifiers without a college degree. In 1943, Myrle K. Wise proudly joined the ranks of the Denver firefighters.

"I would never have got to where I was without Opportunity School's help. I've always told everyone that. They taught you how to study, what to study. They even gave you sample test questions."

Within a few days of joining the department, Myrle knew he wanted to move up; early on, he set his goal to become chief. "I wasn't a follower. I wanted to be a leader. I could see that was a much better life." To accomplish his dream, Myrle realized he'd have to put in his time and capture top scores on upcoming civil service exams. With his determination and Opportunity School's help with the tests, Myrle knew he could succeed.

Over the years, his career included its share of tough times. He worked alongside five men who were killed in the line of duty. One time, he was also administered last rites after a dangerous rescue where it appeared he had succumbed to smoke inhalation. His first year as a "mucker," or probationary fireman, would seem grueling to most. To Myrle, it exemplified heaven. Working every other day on twenty-four-hour shifts, with no days or holidays off for an entire year, Myrle loved the job. He wasn't bothered by the restrictive policy in which the fire and police surgeon made house calls when an employee was absent two consecutive days, to assure the worker was not malingering. Myrle had found his niche. And he thrived.

Steadily, Myrle climbed his way up the firefighter's ladder. Over the next four years, he worked hard, moved up, and eventually became eligible to test for the engineer rank. He returned to Opportunity School and enrolled in another preparatory course. In 1947, he took the engineer exam, scored second among the test-takers, and qualified for one of the department's engineer openings.

Never content to stay in one position long, Myrle moved up to lieutenant in 1948. At age thirty, he was one of the youngest in the department's history to hold this rank. As in the past, Myrle had relied upon Opportunity School to prepare him for the lieutenant's test.

Because their schedules afford them so much time off, most firefighters pursue a second career. Myrle was no exception. Having taken so many classes at Opportunity School, he felt comfortable in education. He had also developed a rapport with the school officials. Starting in the late 1940s, he began teaching classes for Opportunity School on civil defense, preparing citizenry for a nuclear attack, which included the development of a bomb shelter. During the cold war, Myrle became an expert in this area, participating in the development of a nationally distributed film on this subject. Myrle taught this class for many years until the topic no longer held relevance.

In 1950, Myrle headed back to the test room to compete for a captain's position. His success was once again assured when his score qualified him for the advancement. Myrle earned the stripe of assistant chief in 1956. In 1969, he became what was at that time Denver's youngest fire chief. Each time, he secured these positions through civil service tests. His score on the chief's test left no doubt about his competence. Over thirty fire department employees took the exam. A score of seventy or higher was required to pass. Only five qualified. Myrle's score was ninety-six; the next closest was seventy-six.

Over the years, Myrle's ties to Opportunity School remained strong. He not only returned to the school as a student to prepare for upcoming tests, but also worked with EGOS to develop and teach courses. At the conclusion of the era of civil defense classes, he designed and taught a yearlong program training Denver Public

School custodians to be auxiliary firemen. He taught this class for several years.

Denver's Fire Chief

Myrle was young and energetic when he rose to the helm of the Denver fire department. His determination and strength would serve him well. At that time, in 1969, the city's department was nationally rated as dead last, based on criteria such as the department's ability to put out fires and staff morale. Myrle set out to raise this abysmal rating. He devised a plan so every Denver citizen would be within a minute and a half of a fire station. This meant tearing down old fire stations and building new ones in underserved neighborhoods. He was able to accomplish this solely through cost savings, without going to the voters for bond elections.

"When I became chief, our department was very poorly managed. We learned we could close three stations and build two with the cost savings." During Myrle's seventeen-year tenure as chief, the city built seventeen new fire stations.

Many rewards came to Myrle during his career as the Mile High City's fire chief. He was elected chief of chiefs of the International Association of Fire Chiefs, a position that took him to Japan, Germany, and throughout the United States. He developed close friendships with Denver mayor Bill McNichols and former U.S. president Gerald Ford. He also saw his fledgling fire department rise in the national ranks from the last place to first. This, by far, was his greatest achievement.

Personally, Myrle has also been richly rewarded. He has two children, one in Denver and one in California, six grandchildren, and six great-grandchildren. In retirement, Myrle and his wife have divided their months between their Denver home and their condo in San Clemente, California, sharing time with all family members.

Myrle retired in 1987. As Denver's sixth paid fire chief in 100 years, he was the last to acquire the position through the civil service process. Shortly after his departure, citizens voted to change the city charter. Now Denver's fire and police chiefs are appointed by the mayor. Usually adaptable to change, Myrle has voiced reservations about this modification. He questions whether this system ensures that the most qualified persons always fill the positions and whether the appointees are working for the people of the city or for the political enhancement of their boss.

But Myrle knows one institution he doesn't want to see changed. That is Opportunity School. "I know I would never have gotten to where I was without Opportunity School's help…Anyone who really wants to get ahead, that's the place to go. They educate you in what you need to know. It worked for me. I always ended up number one or number two."

As a former city leader well acquainted with Denver's resources, he asserts, "I think Opportunity School is one of the greatest things that has happened in the city and county of Denver. It gives every citizen of this city the opportunity to become proficient in a trade…I'm a real believer in Opportunity School…I consider it one of the greatest institutions we have in the city of Denver."

Author's Note: When I began the interview with Mr. Wise, he focused on the courses he had developed as an EGOS instructor. When I questioned him on his role as a student, he was enthusiastic and had much he wanted to share, especially as he spoke about his rough childhood in Oklahoma. Like so many in this generation, he has overcome much to find success.

MARION KENYON
Aircraft Mechanic, Pilot

"If I hadn't gone to Opportunity School, I would not have reached the talent that I did have and find the success in the maintenance department, where I could pass those trade tests and eventually become a pilot."

As a four-year-old playing in his sandbox in Osborne, Kansas, Marion Kenyon sculpted a large home at the top of a hill, with a long, winding road leading to it. At the bottom of the hill, he carved additional parking spaces for his toy cars. Now, over seventy years later, Marion realizes the dream home he built outside of Parker, Colorado, in 1973 is a replica of his childhood sand sculptures.

Marion's journey from his Kansas childhood to the Parker acreage encountered plenty of turbulence. Nonetheless, his success—fueled by robust determination and helpful boosts from Emily Griffith

Opportunity School—unfolded as a thirty-five-year career with Continental Airlines, culminating as a captain of powerful jets.

It is easy to picture this tall, lean man in his pilot's uniform. But life didn't start out easy for Marion. Born in 1927, he weathered a tough childhood. His parents divorced when he was young, and his father moved to Denver. His alcoholic mother worked during the Depression as a seamstress in a sewing room financed by the government. One day, she decided she could no longer support her young family. After Marion had completed the seventh grade, his mother placed him and his sister, Marguerite, two years his junior, on a bus and sent them to Denver. The children's father, who worked as a Chevrolet mechanic, warmly welcomed them. Surrounded by an extended family of aunts, uncles, and grandparents, the children finally received the love and stability they needed.

Their family happiness and tranquility was short-lived. When Marguerite was sixteen, she and three friends hopped into a 1938 Buick coupe and chased a fire truck down Blake Street. When the fire engine turned onto another street, the car with the teenagers continued straight into a dead end at fifty-five miles per hour. The car jumped the embankment, and all were killed. Heavy-hearted, Marion and his father forged ahead.

Interest in Aviation Is Born

Throughout the years, Marion's father served as his rock and his role model. During World War II, his dad worked at the Denver airport in the modification center, using his mechanical skills to overhaul planes for the war effort. After the war, the senior Mr. Kenyon worked for Continental Airlines. His mechanical and aeronautical skills rubbed off on Marion. "I became interested in aviation because of my father. He was interested in flying. He owned a plane and was a pilot. He let me take lessons and paid for them. As a sixteen-year-old, I had enough time built up [flying] to get my private license," says Marion whose trim body reflects the effects of daily exercise. Quiet, unpretentious, and soft-spoken, he exudes a gentleman-like aura. His full head of gray hair reveals a hint of natural curl. His brown eyes dance with warmth and sincerity.

"I kept going to school, but I never graduated with a diploma from East High School for various reasons," says Marion softly. "I got married for one thing…when I was eighteen."

EGOS: Ticket to a Brighter Future

Soon responsible for a wife and a child, Marion needed to find employment. But first, he wanted a high school diploma or GED. Opportunity School served as his ticket. While obtaining his GED from the school, he learned about its many programs. Tempting as they were, the school's offerings had to be ignored in lieu of supporting his family.

Following in his dad's footsteps, Marion found work at the airport with Western Airlines. "I was basically a helper," he said. "I helped the mechanics. I cleaned the airplanes, pulled them in and out, fueled them." Recognizing that to advance, he needed what was then called an A&E license, he enrolled in a course offered by Denver University (DU) at Sky Ranch, now a closed airport east of the city.

Marion explains, "Today the certification is called A&P, which stands for aircraft and powerplant. Then it was A&E, which stood for aircraft and engines, working on piston airplane engines. When we went to A&P, that included jet engines."

Marion attended DU during the day and worked the 4:00 p.m. to midnight shift. Completing this course, he successfully passed the Federal Aviation Administration (FAA) test for the aircraft portion of the license. Changes followed. Marion and his wife had a second child, Diana, who joined older brother Danny. In addition, Marion moved from Western Airlines to Continental.

To further his career, Marion knew he needed the engine license as well. Financially strapped with a young family, Marion headed to Opportunity School. In 1949, tuition was free, and he enrolled. "I had heard about the aircraft engine course when I took my GED there," says Marion. His new daytime work schedule allowed him to attend Opportunity School four evenings a week. He completed the semester and soon passed the FAA test he needed.

The added certification opened many career doors. It also gave Marion confidence and knowledge to take risks to advance. "Continental had trade tests. All the mechanics hated the trade tests and wouldn't take them. Therefore, they wouldn't move up," Marion said, noting that you had to pass the test in order to be promoted. "No one had taken the trade test, but I took it. And I passed…In fact, I took the test for almost every department." Passing qualified Marion to perform many additional mechanical tasks on the planes.

Marion's training at Opportunity School fueled his accomplishments. "If I hadn't gone to Opportunity School, I would not have reached the talent that I did have and find the success in the maintenance department where I could pass those trade tests and eventually become a pilot."

Marion was flying high. The added certification and his dogged determination unfolded into a long, rich, and prosperous tenure with Continental Airlines. He enjoyed many career advancements, survived several bitter strikes, and witnessed a plethora of human interest stories.

Flying High at Continental

After weathering a mechanics' strike in the 1940s, Marion passed the test that allowed him to become a flight engineer. "I decided after pulling in all those planes in the wintertime, deicing the planes in the cold, and seeing the pilots up in the cockpit drinking coffee, the flight attendants serving them, and here I am out in the cold, pulling in the planes, I thought, 'That's a better life.'" The company was hiring flight engineers for its newly purchased DC-6s. In 1956, Marion was promoted to the cockpit as a flight engineer, seated between the captain and co-pilot.

His new job duties included preparing the plane before takeoff; running all the checklists; monitoring the fuel system, the hydraulic system, and the electric system; and managing all these in flight. Before the pilots boarded, Marion walked around the outside of the plane to check the tires, brakes, static systems, and fuselage. He looked for anything that might be damaged. He also examined the inside, checking all the plane's internal systems, safety equipment, and emergency exits. Prior to takeoff, the flight engineer starts the plane and gets the engines running. Marion's new responsibilities built upon his previous knowledge as a mechanic. He seemed a natural for this new assignment.

While Marion's professional life brought changes, so did his personal life. In the mid-1950s, he and his wife divorced. Approximately a year later, Marion married Marlene, a flight attendant. His new wife gave up her job and raised the four children born to them: Cindy, Joe, Lori, and Lisa.

In 1960, turbulence mounted at work. Continental's flight engineers embarked upon an ill-fated strike. As a lead union member, Marion orchestrated the strike in Denver, and other than providing a nuisance to the company, the walkout accomplished little. After the strike had continued for a year, the company started hiring people off the streets to replace the strikers. Marion had to cast aside his pride and return to work. "I went back to work below the guys they had just hired to replace us. In company seniority I was ahead of them, but in flight seniority I was below them. That made it a bitter pill to swallow." And in the airline industry, flight seniority is golden since it determines the best schedules and best routes. Marion overcame the difficult situation, returned to work, and with his customary determination, forged ahead.

Marion worked as a flight engineer—or second officer, as the position came to be known—for nearly ten years, working on a variety of aircrafts. In the mid-1960s he became a co-pilot, and Continental sent him to school to learn how to fly DC-3s. He worked eight years in that capacity until he became a captain in the early

1970s. Along the way, he sought opportunities to advance, moving up on aircraft and flight schedules. These changes brought more pay and better working conditions.

"I loved every minute of it," Marion states appreciatively.

But still there were challenges. Strikes created particularly tense times. During one mechanics' strike, Marion was flying a DC-10. "I'd always go along and check the plane with the second officer. I saw that the right engine was dripping oil. I called maintenance, and they found the oil line was loose and they thought it was deliberate. The next time I flew, it was the same thing—an oil line was loose—so they tightened it up each time and I went. It turned out, after an investigation, that it was the same mechanic. And on one of my days off, another pilot took the plane out and lost an engine because of oil pressure on the right engine."

This was one of several instances where Marion's mechanical background proved invaluable. Another was more confrontational. Once when he was scheduled to fly a plane from Chicago to Los Angeles, a flight attendant reported she smelled fuel. Marion walked to the back of the plane to check. He concurred and then exited the plane to the back of the aircraft. Seeing the fuselage was wet, he summoned a mechanic.

Marion said, "You better come out here and look at this. This thing is dripping fuel all over the ground, and I think somebody had better see if there is fuel leakage inside the plane."

The mechanic responded indignantly. "Oh, God. You pilots are all the same." He refused to comply with Marion's request.

Marion replied with equal tenacity. "Are you telling me you don't want to check this? You gotta take a look at this. I'm not gonna fly this plane if you're not gonna check it." Seething with anger, Marion returned to the airport terminal. In the meantime, the flight attendants left the plane, declaring they refused to fly if the captain wouldn't go.

Marion's supervisor paged him and said angrily, "Why the hell aren't you gonna fly the plane? If you don't fly the damn plane, I gotta come out there and fly it, and you will have to be in my office on Monday morning."

Marion held firm, stating, "Look, if you want to fly this goddamn plane, you come out and fly it. But no friend of mine is getting on this plane."

Pushing back helped. Marion's supervisor calmed down and asked him to assess the problem. Marion explained the situation, emphasizing the mechanic's unwillingness to check the leak. The supervisor concurred with Marion's assessment, the flight was canceled, and the passengers were rescheduled. When mechanics later examined the plane, they discovered the fuel line to the center engine was leaking and that fuel had accumulated in the bottom of the aircraft. The fuel was close to the electric system. Had the plane flown and the fuel kept leaking, the aircraft would likely have exploded. Fortunately, Marion's expertise as a mechanic, his instincts, and his single-minded focus on passenger safety served the company and its customers well.

After the incident, Frank Lorenzo, the controversial company CEO, called Marion at home and commended him for his efforts. A certificate of commendation, which Marion downplays, also came in the mail.

"I don't think you ought to put that I'm a hero, because I'm not. I was a maintenance guy. I had done inspections, and I had worked on planes. I'd look for stuff like that," states Marion modestly. Yet for the many passengers whom Marion detoured from that precarious plane, this captain would probably be deemed a hero.

Mandatory retirement at age sixty caused Marion to hang up his captain's cap in 1987. To honor his contributions to the company, the Continental marquis at Stapleton International Airport read, "Captain Marion Kenyon is retiring after thirty-five years with Continental." His supervisor researched Marion's career record and discovered he had never had an accident or an incident. "I had absolutely no record of harming an aircraft. I never even blew a tire," says Marion with understated pride. His background in aircraft mechanics and his unwavering commitment to safety contributed to his stellar record.

Like many active, bright people, Marion transitioned to retirement by focusing on long-held interests. For this pilot, newfound freedom involved retreating to the six-car garage attached to his country home to rebuild airplanes and cars. "I've owned airplanes all my life. And I did my own work on my planes. Recently, my son and I bought three Bonanzas, repaired, and sold them." Throughout his time with Continental, Marion bought and restored planes as freelance work. Continuing to pursue this passion in retirement seemed natural. He still uses the license he obtained over fifty years ago at Opportunity School. "I use it all the time to sign off. I've maintained the A&P license all those years."

From his five-acre hilltop home east of Parker, Marion Kenyon has made a safe landing to the good life, a life probably far better than he could ever have imagined as a four-year-old in Kansas. In a significant way, Emily Griffith Opportunity School contributed to this gentle man's career—a career that passed every test with flying colors.

***

Author's Note: *I had known Marion Kenyon for many years; we shared a mutual friendship with Jon Glau. At several of Glau's parties, I had interacted with Marion and heard him describe some of his pilot tales. Unbeknownst to me, he was an Opportunity School graduate. When I embarked upon this book, Jon suggested I interview Marion. I am very grateful for this referral. Marion was recognized as the EGOS outstanding alumnus in 2005.*

EDNA MILLIKEN
Student during Emily's Tenure

"There were a lot of people that hungered for education... The building was plenty old. But I don't think that when you want an education you worry about the building. At least I didn't."

Nearly 1.5 million people can say they have attended Emily Griffith Opportunity School. Edna Milliken is one of the few remaining who can boast that Emily Griffith was her principal.

Born in 1904, Edna attended the school in 1927 and, at the time of the interview, was one of the oldest living alumni of the institution. While her memories of Miss Emily are sketchy, Edna remembers well her early life and the school's impact on it.

Petite and neatly dressed, Edna—known as "Eddie" to family and friends—sits on a gold velvet couch in her east Denver apartment where she lives alone with spunky independence. Her tissue-paper skin is etched with the fine lines of her life's canvas, showing a century of hard work, laughter, and disappointment. Although Edna suffers from macular degeneration, reducing vision in her bright blue eyes, her sharp hearing catches every word spoken, and her attentive mind responds quickly and on target. Her erect posture belies her age.

Edna loves clothing, and her walk-in closet bulges with garments, including formal gowns worn in her younger days when she actively participated in the Eastern Star, a Masonic organization. White dangling earrings, a red leather belt, and white, open-toed lattice shoes accessorize the summer outfit she is wearing of a red and white polka-dot blouse and red skirt.

As Edna settles in to tell her story, she reflects about the unique-ness of Opportunity School. When she attended there in the 1920s, adult education was as common as a two-tailed dog. At that time, if young people dropped out of school, usually because of family economic circumstances, they seldom returned. With Opportunity School offering free tuition and flexible class schedules for adults of all ages, word traveled quickly about this almost-too-good-to-be-true place. People like Edna, who longed for education but had little money, flocked to its doors.

"Students were of various ages, some a lot older than I. It was unusual for adults to go back to school. But you know, there were a lot of people that hungered for education, and I guess when they got a chance they went," Edna says, still marveling more than seventy years later about the unique opportunity the school provided.

Hardship and Challenges

Prior to her time at Opportunity School, Edna experienced much hardship. Loading a reel of history in her mind, Edna remembers detailed events of her early years, playing back vivid memories of an impoverished childhood. Born in Trinidad, Colorado, Edna was the only one of her parents' three children to survive. "I learned to entertain myself," she says in a clear, vibrant voice.

Her father's work as a plasterer caused the family to jump around to communities in Colorado, Nebraska, and Wyoming. Edna recalls living with her parents briefly in a tent because no suitable housing was available. Her father had found work in a new town but couldn't secure housing. As her father moved around chasing work, Edna danced in and out of schools like a gypsy. Education was a luxury that took a backseat to survival and the attainment of food, shelter, and warmth. Edna's chances to benefit from consistent formal schooling were severely impacted until she entered Opportunity School.

Whereas divorce impacts many families today, it was uncommon in Edna's youth. Yet three divorces left their tread marks on Edna's early years. Her parents split up when she was a preteen. The divorce particularly affected Edna as an only child. After that, she seldom saw her father.

On her own, her mother ran a boardinghouse to support herself and Edna. Eventually, her mother remarried a man who operated a water pump for the railroad. Edna and her reconfigured family would move once more when her stepfather's job relocated them to a remote Wyoming community. The nearest school was five miles away, forcing Edna to reluctantly end her education in the ninth grade. It wouldn't be long before Edna would grapple with all too grown-up challenges.

"I left home before I was seventeen. I met and married an engineer on the railroad. I was not old enough to have any sense," Edna says as she touches the soft white curls that frame her face.

Again a divorce would send Edna's life into a tailspin when she and her husband split after five years of marriage. She returned to Wyoming to again live with her mother. Almost like an epidemic, divorce hit their family for a third time when her mother's second marriage also crumbled. Picking up the fragmented pieces of their lives, Edna and her mother settled in Laramie. Too focused on survival, they had no time to feel sorry for themselves. Her mother made ends meet by again running a boardinghouse.

Edna found her first job at Woolworth's. "They paid me $7 per week. You know, honey, it was chicken feed and no chicken could live on it." Other jobs included working in a doctor's office and as a hotel maid.

From the time she was little, Edna was outgoing and friendly. "You know, dear, life is too short not to love people," she reflects. This people-focused philosophy served her well in good times and in bad.

Moving to Denver

Fortunately her mother's boarders recognized Edna's potential: her bright mind and outgoing personality wowed them. They encouraged her to spread her wings. Taking their advice, she journeyed to Denver, temporarily housed with an aunt, and attended Parks College. "I went one month to Parks and I couldn't afford it." Soon she heard about Opportunity School and headed there because the tuition was free.

Loading another reel of history in her mind, Edna recalls the physical surroundings of her newfound school. "There was nothing at the school but the bare necessities. The building was plenty old. But I don't think that when you want an education you worry about the building. At least I didn't," she explains with the pragmatic attitude characteristic of her generation.

With her welcome worn out at her aunt's, Edna needed housing. "I went to the lady who helped students get jobs. I told her I needed a place to stay, and she placed me with her sister and mother...I got $3.25 per week plus board and room...That wasn't bad in those days," says Edna, explaining that she did light housework in exchange for food, shelter, and pay.

Class Acts

At Opportunity School, Edna focused on practical training and studied English, spelling, shorthand, and typing. She knew she needed skills for employment in order to support herself as soon as possible. "I had the most wonderful English teacher. She gave me worlds of encouragement. She wanted me to finish high school, go to college, and become an attorney. She said I had a logical mind and would make a wonderful attorney. Of course, that was unheard of because I didn't have money to buy oats for a night mare!" And in those days, pursuing a law degree was a far reach for most, and particularly for women.

Living in northwest Denver, Edna rode the streetcar to school each day, traveling with another girl from the neighborhood. One day, her friend asked Edna to accompany her to the Orpheum Theater for a chorus tryout. Edna agreed, recalling that, after her friend tried out, the man in charge kept calling for more prospects to come forward. "The pay was $25 per week. That was a lot of money for me…So I finally got up and went to the stage. I had never had a dance lesson in my life, but I loved to dance…and I loved music. I had a natural ear for music but never had a lesson. So I got up, and he took me. It was dancing and singing. They had 200 girls in the theater, and I was one of eight chosen," Edna states proudly.

The nine-performance production lasted one week and deepened Edna's interest in music. She decided to pursue voice lessons. Her friend took lessons from the choir director at Grace Church, so Edna tagged along one day and bartered with him. He agreed to give her lessons for a nominal fee, in exchange for her joining the church choir.

She sandwiched in music activities with school studies at Opportunity School for six months, long enough to obtain the skills she needed to launch her beyond manual labor. Out of money, she utilized the school's job placement services to secure work as a clerk at Purple Sage Oil Company. She left Opportunity School, grateful for its comprehensive help. "The education at Opportunity School gave me confidence, dear, because it taught me things I needed to know." The free tuition, housing referral, and job placement assistance were invaluable as well.

Life after Opportunity School

Edna's brief stay at Opportunity School now seems like a speck of time in her century-long life. Opportunity's doors opened to her at a critical point, enabling her to rise above a poverty-stricken past and nudging her forward to a more optimistic future.

While her work life blossomed, Edna's personal life also bloomed. She met a tenor in the church choir, who, after seeing Edna for the first time, told his friend, "I'm gonna marry that girl." In October 1928, Edna married her suitor and continued to work until they had their first child in 1931. After that, she never worked again outside the home. A second daughter came in 1933.

A widow since 1975, Edna exudes an enthusiastic love for life. She has enjoyed music as a lifelong mainstay and readily shares her talent with others. "I take my uke and play old songs and entertain…I'm very lucky I haven't gotten this squeaky old voice that old people get…I sing solos, and I get everybody to sing, too." She also recalls organizing a hillbilly singing group in 1958 as part of her Eastern Star activities and taking their musical show on the road to rest homes and hospitals.

Edna's song of life has carried many soulful and joyous tunes and has played many verses throughout the years—sometimes light and lifting, other times burdened with poverty and struggles. She says, "This year, my memory is slipping. It is going out of gear." However, as she replays tales of events that happened years ago, vivid recollections easily surface.

And her historical perspective related to adult education provides a refreshingly grateful attitude for a concept most take for granted today. "I always thought Opportunity School was a wonderful place because it gave the fellow who didn't have the money an education. I think education shouldn't be limited to people who have money."

Her former principal, Emily Griffith, would most certainly agree.

***

Author's Note: Judy Butler, an EGOS employee, told me I needed to interview her "Aunt Eddie" for my book. I'm so grateful for this recommendation. Sharp, fun, and full of life, Edna was a delight. Edna passed away in July 2005.

H. GORDON GATES
Business Leader

*"I don't think I could have ever done what I've been
able to accomplish if I hadn't gone to Opportunity
School...I can't compliment or praise
Opportunity School enough."*

Gordon Gates returned home from World War II in 1945 with
every intention of becoming a physician. His extensive training
and experience in the U.S. Army Medical Corp, where he helped
save lives in the makeshift 1,000-bed hospital at Iwo Jimo, focused him on
a future career in medicine. "After coming from the army, having worked
a year in surgery, I enjoyed it. I loved the anatomy," says Gordon in a raspy
but spirited voice. The words roll off his tongue in a fast pace. Although

eighty years old, Gordon thinks fast, talks fast, and moves fast. Long before the term *multitasking* became fashionable, he seems to have mastered it.

Of medium build with grayish-white hair, Gordon conveys the impression that his mind moves more swiftly than the words can shoot from his mouth. He wears a sapphire blue shirt with white window-pane checks. The blue garment echoes the color of his eyes, increasing their vibrancy. His company's name, Gates Concrete Forming Systems, is embroidered over the left pocket in heavy white thread with bold lettering. The weight of several note cards, a pen, and a six-inch ruler bulges the pocket.

World War II

Gordon and his twin brother, Bob, served in the war side by side. They shared a foxhole in Iwo Jimo, dodging Japanese gunfire, sewing up battle scars, and witnessing carnage as some 21,000 Japanese and 7,000 Americans lost their lives on that eight-square-mile island in one of the bloodiest battles of the war. Both returned home safely to the welcoming arms of their wives, parents, and four siblings.

Prior to the war, in the 1930s, Gordon's father had invented and patented a revolutionary concrete form tie. A few years later, his construction company started to take off, but in the early 1940s, with all available steel directed toward the war effort, his business lapsed into a coma.

When Gordon returned from the Pacific in March 1945, his father supported his goal of becoming a doctor but encouraged him to work in the family business until he was to start school in the fall. Both Gordon's older brother and his twin had already joined the company, which was once again booming. "During the war, this country did not build houses, did not build cars, did not build refrigerators...After the war, there was a tremendous surge of construction, starting in 1946," explains Gordon, often illustrating his points with a ballpoint pen on a yellow-lined tablet. He draws as quickly as he talks.

Joining the Family Business, Enrolling at EGOS

Gordon soon got hooked on the family business and shelved his dream of becoming a doctor. "I was making pretty good money. I figured I had at least four years of college, four years of medical school, and two years of residency—at least ten years of schooling ahead. I got to thinking, 'There's a bright future right here,'" says Gordon, gesturing to his surroundings as he sits in the paneled conference room at Gates and Sons, Inc. Rolled, transparent sheets of blueprints rest on the conference table before him.

Always good in math and architectural drafting, Gordon appeared to be a natural for the construction business. His father had high expectations and encouraged his sons to develop their talents. They joined the carpenters' union and became journeymen carpenters, which entailed two nights of training for four years at Emily Griffith Opportunity School. Highly motivated and eager to learn, Gordon rounded out his weekly schedule with two more nights of classes at EGOS, taking drafting and math. During the day, he worked in the family business. "That was tough, four nights per week for four years, plus working for my father." During this time, he and his wife, Nida, started their family. Eventually, they had three children: Gloria, Gordie, and Debbie.

While the schedule and time demands were tough, Gordon credits his success to the education he received at Emily Griffith. "What I learned at Opportunity School were the tools I needed to do what I'm doing. I learned drafting, I learned math, I learned carpentry…The teachers were great: very fine, fair, and well educated. Tuition was free. All we had to do was put out the effort."

Growing the Company

Putting out the effort is a consistent trait that runs in the Gates family gene pool. Together, the elder Gates, his three sons, and their mother, who maintained the books, grew the business. As the company matured, changes evolved. When Gordon's father turned seventy, he retired. Oldest brother Bud became the president. Gordon specialized in sales, and his twin brother, Bob, eventually caught the entrepreneurial bug, launching his own successful company, Sure Void. In the meantime, Gates and Sons, Inc., churned along successfully, swelling to an international operation. Gordon's responsibilities expanded to also head up the company's research and development arm. In time, Gordon assumed the company's reins. In 1990, his brother Bud retired and Gordon bought out his portion of the business, becoming the company's third president.

He became the leader of a business that has made a major impact on Denver in the past and, under Gordon's able vision and management, is poised to do so far into the future. The operation employs between 120 and 140 people. Standing at the intersection of Bayaud and Fox streets in south-central Denver, one can see a Gates building on every corner as well as up and down the better part of four blocks. In addition, the company owns and operates out of a large piece of property on Tejon Street.

The company's bread and butter continues to be the original concrete form tie invented by Gordon's father. Most major Denver construction projects have used the Gates concrete form, including Invesco Field at Mile High, Denver International Airport, and the city's convention center. Gates inventions are used all over the United States as well as Canada, Japan, and the northern portion of South America.

Although he has his successor in training, Gordon has no plans of retiring soon. He has reached a point where his work is more enjoyable than ever. Buffered from the front-line problems, Gordon now concentrates on big-picture issues and enjoys the people with whom he has surrounded himself.

With eight decades under his belt, Gordon has also reached a point where he is reflecting on his past. As part of their sixtieth wedding anniversary celebration, he and his wife, joined by their son and daughter-in-law, journeyed to Iwo Jimo, a pilgrimage that resurrected a wide array of emotions.

Gordon has now achieved that golden age where he unabashedly shares his opinions, whether popular or politically correct. One robust view relates to funding for vocational education. When he hears about budget cuts in this area, his blood boils. "I think not everybody financially or mentally can go to college. But when we do away with our trade schools or cut them way back, we are just hurting our workforce…We have dollars for swimming pools, track, and sex education and then they turn around and cut funding to help young people learn a trade…There are a lot of good jobs out there in the trades," Gordon says with combined irritation and evangelistic zeal.

Reviewing the past includes reflecting upon his former dream of becoming a doctor. "I have never been sorry that I did not go into medicine…I enjoy what I do."

However, Gordon thanks his lucky stars for Emily Griffith. "I don't think I could have ever done what I've been able to accomplish if I hadn't gone to Opportunity School…Had I not gone to Opportunity School, I think I would have been handicapped in my job. I can't compliment or praise Opportunity School enough."

With a blueprint, rather than a stethoscope, Gordon Gates has made his mark.

Author's Note: *I tried for over a year to arrange an interview with Mr. Gates. Each phone conversation we had was pleasant, but he was always too busy to meet, asking that I call him back a few days or weeks later. Most of our phone chats were fairly long, as the topics often diverted to current events of the day, such as the war in Iraq or funding cuts for education. I found his strong "tell it like it is" opinions refreshing. Just when I was about to give up, he worked me into his schedule.*

JOHN TEGEL
Brewer, Farmer

"The teachers were real good. For a person who has limited opportunity as far as school, there is no better place in the world to further your education."

John Tegel is a man of intriguing contrasts. He spent more than thirty years brewing beer yet never drank a drop. At eighty-three, he has accumulated much wealth, but he still mows and bales his hay fields and handpicks apples from his orchard to sell at a roadside stand. John last set foot in Emily Griffith Opportunity School in the 1950s, but he remembered the institution when he wrote his will in 1991.

Sharing his story from his fifteen-acre farm on the northwest edge of Arvada, Colorado, John wears a blue chambray shirt, a royal blue down vest, and denim jeans. His clothing emphasizes his rich blue eyes. He has a full head of white hair, and his thin, slightly stooped body shows his eighty-three years.

John lives simply. His farm and home look as if the calendar has been turned back thirty years; his surroundings are richly saturated in the past. An old Ford tractor that could have been on the 1960s TV show *The Real McCoys* stands in solitude like a well-worn toy abandoned in a sunny yard. With new housing developments surrounding his land, his farm is as out of place as a single cornstalk standing tall in a yard of manicured grass.

Finding Work, Attending School

John attended Emily Griffith Opportunity School shortly after starting work at Coors Brewery in the late 1940s. Home from World War II where he had seen action as a navy gunman in the Pacific battles of Guadalcanal and Okinawa, he eagerly embarked on his postwar life. He narrowed his employment options to public service utilities, the phone company, and Adolph Coors Brewery—three solid companies he believed would provide job security and good benefits. Ultimately, he chose Coors because it was closest to home.

John started as a tank liner at Coors, putting plastic liners in containers that held the beer, and he eventually moved to supervisor of brewery control. A recall to the navy during the Korean conflict, where he was assigned to prepare warehoused ships for return to battle, briefly interrupted his early employment.

After his second tour of duty, John returned to his management position at Coors. Back at work, he realized he needed help in supervising people. He had an excellent work ethic but needed people skills. To enhance his ability, he enrolled in the Emily Griffith class, "Psychology of Working with People."

"The class helped me. I was scared to face the public, to talk to employees," John admits. "I remember there were about thirty in the class, and the instructor, Pat Davis, said that after the second session more than half would quit because the class was not about understanding others. It was about understanding ourselves."

Successful in his first course, John enrolled in two additional Emily Griffith classes: electrical motor rewinding, to help with the mechanical functions of his job, and Spanish, to aid in communication with his Spanish-speaking employees. He was satisfied with every class and later discovered that many principles covered in the psychology class were also included in a Dale Carnegie course taught at Coors.

"I thought Emily Griffith was the best thing in the world for people who wanted to learn something. The teachers were real good. For a person who has had limited opportunity, as far as school, there is no better place in the world to further your education," John says appreciatively.

Developing a Work Ethic, Enjoying Simple Things

John was born in a coal mine camp outside Rock Springs, Wyoming. At age three, he moved with his family to Arvada. His father's untimely death in the Leyden coal mine caused him to drop out of school in the eighth grade.

A typical member of the World War II generation, John developed a self-sacrificing work ethic. He worked thirty-four years at Coors, lived conservatively, and slowly accumulated an estate of seven rental properties, farmland, and diversified investments.

Married twice and a widower since 1978, John now has a son, a grandson, and twin great-granddaughters, all of whom live in California. Feeling his heirs would be well provided for, he elected to also remember Opportunity School in his will. When asked why he chose Emily Griffith even though he hadn't attended there in some fifty years, he replies in a raspy voice weakened by age and the effects of a major stroke, "I can't see a better place to put it. I felt awfully good about this school."

John enjoys the simple things in life: a doe and her fawns frolicking in his orchard, fragrant with the smells of ripened apples; the changing colors of crunchy fall leaves; the unexpected pleasure of neighbors stopping by to say hello. His daily routine includes watching *As the World Turns* with his noon meal and listening to the boisterous rhythm of *Wheel of Fortune* with supper.

When commended on his ambitious work ethic and self-sacrificing behaviors, he dodges the praise and says in his trademark, understated way, "Time was used properly. I took advantage of what was at hand. I used to best advantage what was there."

Opportunity School was one such resource. John Tegel, a man of contrasts, jokingly calls himself weird. Most others would call him wise.

***

Author's Note: I called early one fall morning explaining my book project and requesting a future interview. He suggested I come that very morning. I dropped everything and drove into his yard two hours later. My time with him included a tour of his farm. I left with a sense of appreciation that there are still people like him in this world.

FLORA GASSER
Community Activist, Writer, Recruiter

"There isn't anything I wouldn't do for this school.
I found friends there who became like a second family."

"Denver is sentimental about Opportunity School. It is an original school. Nobody had ever heard of a school like Opportunity School, and it has touched so many lives." From her brick ranch home in southwest Denver, Flora Gasser passionately describes Opportunity School and Emily Griffith's legendary presence in Denver and in the Gasser family. Miss Griffith impacted four generations of this clan. "It has been a godsend to immigrants," Flora continues. "People…who didn't have an education and school dropouts who never had a chance…The school is the heart of Denver. That is the place where all the misplaced people go, looking for an opportunity."

Flora, a Denver native of Italian descent and former Emily Griffith Opportunity School student, speaks from experience. Ninety years old, her stature reduced by age, Flora walks tentatively with the assistance of a copper-colored metal cane. Weak in body, but strong in mind and spirit, she vividly recalls memories of the school. Severely hearing impaired, Flora focuses intently on the lips of her conversation partner to catch every word spoken. When she laughs, which is often, she reveals a full set of white teeth, the front two separated by a slight gap.

Family Ties to Emily Griffith

Prior to founding Opportunity School in 1916, Emily Griffith taught in an elementary school. One of her students was Lou Gasser, the father of Flora's husband. When Lou was about to exit from school at the completion of the eighth grade, as was customary at that time, Miss Griffith visited his mother at their home. She advised Mrs. Gasser to help her son start his own business. Clever, creative, and highly self-directed, but difficult to get along with, Lou appeared to be a poor candidate to work for someone else. In fact, Emily encouraged his mother to do whatever she could, even mortgage her home, to subsidize the start of a small business.

Following Emily's advice, the elder Mrs. Gasser set up a shop for Lou in the back of their home. But Lou's education didn't stop there. He followed Miss Griffith to Opportunity School, the school she founded for adults, to develop skills in shop classes. Lou's creativity paid off. He started a business that designed bronze tablets and cremation burial urns. With cremation more accepted in California, Lou eventually moved the company west, where it became a thriving business.

"The family owes everything to Emily Griffith. Without her, the guy would have been a bum. He couldn't get along with anyone," states Flora of her father-in-law. A soft buzz beeps from the temporarily malfunctioning hearing aid in her left ear.

Opportunity School is a long-standing Gasser family tradition. Many of Lou's descendants followed his lead and went to

Opportunity School. His son Ray, Flora's husband, studied metals and was invited to teach at the school, though he declined. Flora's daughter, Raymona Evenson, participated in the school's parent education and preschool program at Doull School with her three sons, Chris, Kent, and Brad. Kent also attended art classes at Opportunity School.

"I took a journalism class offered by Opportunity School at West High School while attending St. Joseph High. That helped me get a job at the *Denver Post* as a reporter. Mr. Frederick Bonfils hired me, and he always called me the kid reporter." Her big brown eyes look intently through glasses with trifocal lenses. She worked at the *Post* for around six months before resigning to accept a position with a Denver neighborhood paper.

Flora continued to seek out Opportunity School to hone her skills. In 1932, at age twenty, she decided to take a Dictaphone class at the school. "I went to the school to enroll. Sitting outside was a blond boy, handsome, light-skinned, and pretty. I thought he looked like an angel. We said hello to each other. I went in the school and made arrangements to study Dictaphone, and when I came out, he was still sitting there and said that he had been waiting for me. I hurried away to catch my streetcar, and he followed me the two or three blocks until I boarded the streetcar to go home. I was so scared. As I left, he said, 'Good-bye, I will be waiting for you at school tomorrow.' Well, I was so scared, I never did go back," laughs Flora.

Returning to Opportunity School

In fact, Flora didn't return until 1986, when she was in her seventies. She had been politically connected and active in the community. With a change in Denver mayors, she was making a transition in her life. As a writer and community volunteer, she had served on several mayoral-appointed boards and had many local contacts. She sought new ways to challenger her active mind. Opportunity School seemed the obvious place to go.

Self-described as terrified of the microwave, Flora enrolled in culinary classes at a time when consumer cooking courses were thriving. Each week, she brought her favorite staff homemade goodies such as tasty Italian cookies, rich with a buttery flavor, the outside coated with coconut and filled with tangy apricot jam. Sometimes she shared freshly picked garden flowers such as lipstick pink phloxes and lilacs fragrant with the fresh smell of spring.

Although somewhat older than the "traditional" student, Flora felt most welcome at Emily Griffith, proving the school's motto, providing education "for all who wish to learn" is tried and true. Successful and satisfied with her first class, she enrolled in several others, including "Floral Design," "Cooking Lite," "Healthy Cooking for the Heart," "Garnishing," "Chinese Cooking," and "Cake Decorating."

Championing the School

Alert and threaded with a sense of activism, Flora noted that many improvements needed to be made for the school. Not one to use her political connections for personal enhancement, Flora nonetheless shamelessly advocated for causes in which she believed. Her first crusade aimed at making the public bus system better for Opportunity School students. She contacted a young man she knew who was politically ambitious and recently elected to the RTD board and asked for his help. Through their joint efforts, directions to Opportunity School were printed on bus schedules, and the routes of selected RTD buses were altered to include stops on Welton Street.

This victory spurred her onward. Next, Flora contacted her longtime friend Bill Roberts, who was serving as a department head for the mayor. She told him that Opportunity School students were leaning against the building in the hot sun eating their lunches. With her sweet voice, she asked, "Wouldn't it be nice if the students had trees and a place to sit while they ate their lunches?" Within a short time, a letter came from the City of Denver indicating that trees, benches, garbage cans, ashtrays, new cement, and an underground sprinkling system would be installed on the school's west side.

Flora whipped into action one more time when she learned that Denver cable magnate Bill Daniels had made a large donation to a private Denver university. She knew Daniels well, having volunteered for his gubernatorial campaign many years earlier. His campaign headquarters were near Opportunity School, and Flora felt Daniels' background paralleled that of many Opportunity School students. She wrote him a heartfelt letter asking for financial support to the school. Weeks before his death, Daniels sent her a letter committing future foundation assistance.

Championing school improvements and taking classes seemed to nourish Flora's creative energies. While at Opportunity School, she wrote and published two books of poetry. She donated proceeds from her books to the school for student scholarships. "I remember one day a young man had to leave class because he didn't have money to pay the fees. Another time, one of my favorite fellow students, Mary, said she could not return next semester because of lack of money. I wanted to help people like that."

Without a doubt, Flora positively impacted the school. When asked of the school's impact on her, she says, "Attending there was one of the smartest things I ever did in my life. A whole new world opened for me." Gesturing with her large hands, she says she not only learned to conquer the microwave, she also developed better eating habits. But most important, she formed wonderful friendships.

"There isn't anything I wouldn't do for the school. That school was always there to help people who needed help. I found friends there who became a second family. It's almost as if Emily blessed me when I walked in that door…Emily's spirit is still there. Her spirit hovers over the school."

A few years ago, Flora learned again that the ties between the Gassers and Emily Griffith are eternal. To her delight, Flora discovered Emily Griffith is buried next to her husband's Grandmother

Gasser (the woman Emily had visited so long ago) at Fairmount Cemetery—*almost like family.*

***

Author's Note: *I was fortunate to be one of Flora's favorites at EGOS. Each week she came to school, she lavished me with fresh goodies from her kitchen or flowers from her garden. We became dear friends, and she seemed like my "Denver mother." Flora passed away July 10, 2003.*

Two
Prosperity and Optimism
1955–1975

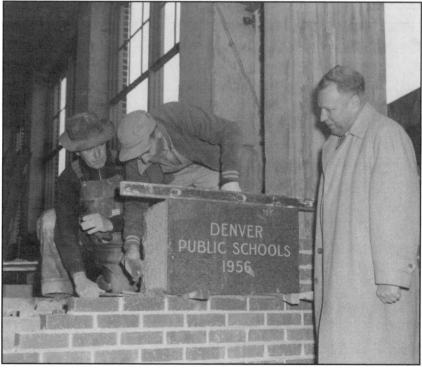

After forty years, the Longfellow building was razed, and in 1956, the cornerstone was laid for a new building addition. Howard L. Johnson, EGOS principal from 1944 to 1960, is at right.

I n the decades between 1955 and 1975, Emily Griffith Opportunity
School mirrored the changes of the larger world. The postwar
period brought prosperity to the country and the school. A sense of
optimism enveloped the nation and swept through the halls of Emily
Griffith. In the 1960s, the country focused on social programs, promoted
civil rights, and became entangled in a controversial war. For the school,
this two-decade period proved to be among its best because facilities
expanded, programs flourished, and new ideas abounded.

In 1955, the Longfellow School was razed to make room for a four-
story building at 13th and Welton Streets, nearly doubling EGOS's
classroom capacity. The ambitious construction project also included
industrial shops and a building on Glenarm Street to house the KRMA
television studios (Channel 6), which fell under the auspices of EGOS.
With the completion of construction in 1956, the EGOS campus
comprised an entire city block.

In the 1950s, Denver's population boomed—to 493,837 by 1960,
according to the census that year—and so did the enrollment at EGOS.

*New building construction, funded by the Denver Public Schools, expanded
the school campus to an entire city block, encompassing the area between
12th and 13th Streets and Welton and Glenarm Streets.*

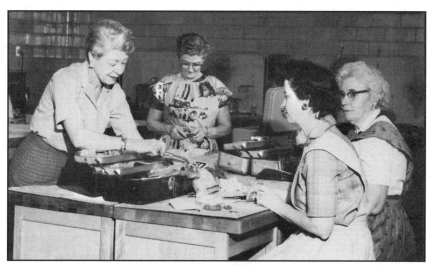

Program offerings expanded to include many hobby courses.
These students are learning jewelry making.

Full- and part-time faculty grew to 550, and the school offered more than 300 subjects. As self-development and hobby courses proliferated, annual enrollment ballooned to 43,000. Waiting lists climbed to 3,700. By 1959, nearly 597,000 students had passed through Emily's doors since 1916, an attendance total that surpassed the city's population.

National companies, such as Martin Company, Sundstrand, Stanley Aviation, and Dow Chemical, identified the school's extensive training program as a recruitment tool in deciding to relocate to Denver. Time, Inc. cited EGOS as the deciding factor in its move to Denver. In 1960–1961 alone, 192 local firms

The school's training programs served as a recruitment tool in urging companies to relocate to Denver.

asked that their personnel be trained by the school. In the 1966–1967 school year, companies sent over 1,500 separate letters requesting training for their employees.

Businesses reciprocated their support by donating equipment and serving on EGOS's advisory committees. The U.S. Naval Reserve presented a Skyway Jet to the school. Other donations included a new Zenith color television and a new 1968 Chrysler Imperial. Some 1,800 business and community people also provided program input to 90 advisory committees.

The school enjoyed many contributions from businesses, including a new 1968 Chrysler Imperial presented to EGOS principal Russell Casement from the Chrysler Corporation.

Despite the growth, budget issues surfaced. In 1957, adult education consumed 5 percent of the Denver Public Schools' fiscal pie. Opportunity School's operating costs hovered at $1.4 million. A proposal to charge tuition first surfaced in 1957 but was eventually defeated by the Denver Public Schools Board of Education.

In the early 1960s, conflicts churned over higher education and Opportunity School's place in the puzzle. Junior colleges expanded. When Metropolitan State College was founded in 1965 and

Community College of Denver in 1968, many people questioned the impact of these neighboring institutions on EGOS. School officials and supporters feared for EGOS's budget support. The cost of running the school had become increasingly burdensome to the Denver Public Schools, and legislators debated state aid for EGOS. Denver legislator Roy Romer said, "Opportunity School should get the same aid as Colorado's six junior colleges."[1] His reasoning seemed sound since, in 1961, EGOS clocked 1.7 million hours of instruction, a number that rivaled the combined total of 2.1 million hours amassed by students in the state's six junior colleges.

In 1972, after wrestling with EGOS's place in the educational system, the legislature established funding for area vocational schools (AVS). EGOS and six other schools were designated as AVS facilities. Others were located in Fort Collins, Boulder, Aurora, Alamosa, near Cortez, and near Delta. This legislation cemented the school's place in the state budget—but at a level below community colleges. As a result, EGOS started the 1974 school year as an area vocational school.

The school's steadfast adherence to vocational training paved the way for EGOS to be designated as an area vocational school in 1974.

The school's reputation continued to reach far-flung corners of the world. Visitors from Australia, Burma, Pakistan, and Zanzibar soaked up the school's philosophy in hopes of implementing the same in their homelands. During 1966–1967, the school's fiftieth year, more than one thousand people from more than thirty countries visited the EGOS campus.

Exploration in outer space created a greater need for advanced technology and electronics. In response, EGOS launched an electronics technician program in 1961.

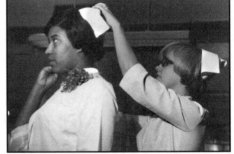

At the same time, the need for trained workers in the medical field also expanded. Between 1947 and 1967, enrollment in this field skyrocketed from 194 to 5,214. The school began a medical assistant program in 1960, and the dental assistant program expanded to include a state-of-the-art dental clinic built in 1966. In 1967, the school established a separate health occupations department.

The health occupations area grew significantly between 1947 and 1967.

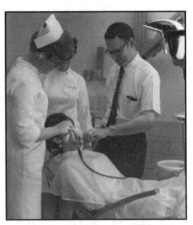

The aircraft training program also soared during this period. In 1968, it moved to enlarged facilities at Stapleton Airport, and by that year, 850 licensed aircraft mechanics had graduated from the program.

Social programs in the 1960s, such as the War on Poverty, ushered in financial support and incentives to train the unemployed. To address poverty, the

The school built a state-of-the-art dental lab in 1966 to train dental assistants.

school offered courses on using commodity foods, stretching a limited budget, and parenting for residents in low-income neighborhoods.

Aircraft mechanics students enjoyed their new and enlarged facility at Stapleton Airport that opened in 1968.

EGOS also started classes to train welfare recipients as homemaker aides and home health assistants.

As racial tensions and social unrest erupted throughout the country, EGOS's corridors resembled the United Nations: harmonious, respectful, and diverse. The student body included blacks, whites, Asians, Hispanics, and immigrants from many different countries. While mandatory desegregation in the 1970s led to racial tension and violence in the Denver school district, EGOS—fully integrated since its inception—encountered few problems. The multicultural student body contributed to the school's success.

During these years, people in the United States also became more concerned about literacy. Nationally nearly 10 million adults were functionally illiterate. In 1970, Denver's census report revealed more than 3,100 adults over the age of twenty-five had never attended school. Nearly 61,000 had earned an eighth-grade education or less, and over 110,000 possessed no more than an eleventh-grade education. Between 1968 and 1969, EGOS boasted 1,646 registrations in academic classes below the ninth grade and 4,751 in high school classes.

Responding to the needs of the city's undereducated, the school expanded its GED courses and testing. During the 1974–1975 school year, EGOS offered GED preparation classes at its main campus as well as in many community centers throughout the city. In 1974, 32 percent of the state's GED tests were administered at EGOS. Nearly 2,400 GED exams were administered in twenty-six testing centers.

Courses, such as power sewing, emphasized · wage-earning skills leading to self-sufficiency.

As the school expanded, so did its teachers' clout, enabling them to negotiate an attractive salary package. In 1970, the EGOS teachers' union, Local 203, negotiated a settlement that included a $7,140 starting salary for a beginning teacher with a high school diploma and five years' trade experience. A starting teacher with a bachelor's degree earned $8,400, and one with a master's captured $13,580. By contrast, the average salary for all Colorado teachers, regardless of experience, was $7,761.

A diverse student body learned in a harmonious, respectful environment.

For many, EGOS served as a launching pad for further education.

In 1972, EGOS celebrated a milestone when its one-millionth student walked through the doors. That same year, Congress passed the Title IX education amendments, broadening opportunities for both men and women. This legislation enabled and encouraged people to pursue careers beyond those traditionally limited by gender. Now men were free to study nursing, for example, and women could pursue aircraft mechanics.

A positive educational experience at Emily's school often proved to be a launching pad for further education. To pave the way for easy entry into college-level courses, EGOS and the Community College of Denver developed cooperative agreements in 1974. These arrangements allowed EGOS students to transfer to the community college to earn an associate's degree. Eventually, such agreements were developed with all metro-area community colleges.

Class Acts

The school's tremendous impact on Denver and Colorado was undeniable. To recognize its visionary founder, the Colorado State Senate named Emily Griffith an outstanding Colorado woman in 1975 and enshrined her portrait in a stained-glass window, hung at the state capitol in 1976.

In the years between 1955 and 1975, the school welcomed uniquely diverse students who benefited from Emily Griffith's vision of providing free adult education. This section profiles nine of these remarkable individuals.

Note

1. Jack Gaskie, "Legislators Explore Opportunity School," *Rocky Mountain News,* July 14, 1962, 7.

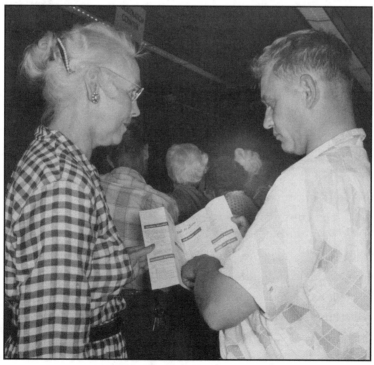

Many students benefited from the school's philosophy of providing "education for all who wish to learn."

MYRON GOOCH
Business Owner

"Oh, man. Had I not gone to Opportunity School, I think, what would I be doing? I probably make more in a trade than had I gone to college."

The economy softened in 1962, and Myron Gooch needed to "keep himself on wheels." Twenty-five years old with a growing family, he worked as a custodian at Martin Marietta from 5:00 p.m. to 1:00 a.m. When his car started to make suspicious noises, Myron didn't panic. He took action. Because he lacked the cash to pay for car repairs, Myron enrolled in the Emily Griffith Opportunity School auto mechanics program to learn how to fix his vehicle. Tuition was free for Denver residents at the time. Myron soon discovered both an economical way to maintain his car and a route to a revenue-generating skill.

Developing Skills in Auto Mechanics

"I was curious about cars. I wanted to know how they worked. I couldn't afford to have anyone work on mine. I never thought I would be good enough to work on anyone else's car. I decided to go to school to learn to work on my own," says Myron. The husky man with gray-peppered hair smiles easily and often and enjoys deep belly laughs, especially when poking fun at himself. Opportunity School forever changed this good-natured, hardworking man's life.

Once he discovered his talent for auto mechanics, Myron attended Opportunity School for three years. "Opportunity School is what it says. It gave me an opportunity to learn a trade. I wasn't the smartest student, but I was the most persistent. Oh, man. Had I not gone to Opportunity School, I think, what would I be doing? I probably make more money in a trade than had I gone to college. Not to put down an education. You can get a trade and still do good," says Myron. "I can't begin to explain how it helped. I got a totally free education."

To succeed, Myron faced and overcame a variety of challenges, not the least of which was juggling work, school, and family obligations. "I got off at Martin at 1:00 at night. I got three to four hours' sleep, went to Emily Griffith during the day from 8:00 to 12:00, and then slept in the afternoon again before going to work—split-shift sleeping. It was hard. I lost a lot of sleep. Sometimes I got so tired I slept all day on the weekend to catch up."

Employment in His New Field

Fate added to his struggles. The economy worsened in 1965, and Myron was laid off at Martin Marietta. However, the Fort Worth, Texas, native, one of nine children, had developed resiliency. Still attending Opportunity School part-time, he utilized the school's job placement office and landed work at Dean Buick. He was hired to wash cars, and he vividly remembers his first day on the job, removing more than ten inches of wet March snow from each vehicle. "I washed cars for three months. I worked hard. I give all in everything I do."

His work ethic began to pay off. Within twelve weeks, the shop foreman promoted him to the service area, where he would check in and road test new cars, put on hubcaps, and prepare vehicles for the showroom. Three months later, he advanced to working on "old" cars, customer vehicles needing repairs. Initially, he worked in a salaried position but soon moved to a more lucrative flat rate. Three months later, he was promoted to transmission work.

"I learned how to rebuild five different types of transmissions in one month. The guy who worked on transmissions was retiring, and I had to learn fast," he says. "I remained in that job for thirteen-and-a-half years."

Myron readily acknowledges that success entails more than luck. "When I went to Dean Buick, I moved up so fast because I had good work habits: never complain, do the job they give you to do, do it with a smile. I had customers who came up to me and said, 'I want you to work on my car.' They see how you work."

Myron's boss wasn't the only one to recognize his determination and talent. In 1970, his former Emily Griffith teacher, Colo Halmi, who by then was a school administrator, enlisted Myron to teach night classes at Opportunity School. "He didn't ask me. He told me I should come," Myron states matter-of-factly. "Colo was my hero. He had the greatest impact on me. He was a good teacher. When you have a good teacher, you are motivated to learn. If anybody could teach me, it was Colo. He had charisma. He wasn't that much older than me. We could relate. He was my brother." Myron accepted the teaching job and continued to work days at Dean Buick while teaching auto mechanics two evenings per week.

Myron's home life prospered as well. He and his wife purchased a new home in 1970 to accommodate their family of five children. When their brand-new dwelling had no window coverings, Myron enrolled in the Opportunity School drapery class to learn how to sew.

"I made the drapes, measured them, and hung them. Not one drapery rod fell out of the wall. They came out neat. When they closed, they closed," Myron says with obvious pride. "We also purchased a Winnebago motor home in 1972 and I made all the window coverings for that. In addition, I took the Opportunity School upholstery class and upholstered a chair."

Perhaps experiencing the many benefits of Opportunity School firsthand inspired Myron to become an instructor there. In 1980, he left Dean Buick to teach full-time. To keep his hand in the mechanics business, Myron had also built an extra garage behind his house for freelance work. "I made more money at home from 3:00 to 10:00 than I did teaching. I made more money in a week there than I did teaching all summer." While Myron enjoyed teaching from 1980 to 1985, the lucrative automotive trade eventually lured him away. "I quit because I could make more money in industry. Plus in teaching you had to go to school and take all those classes."

Starting His Business

In 1985, Myron opened Gooch's Transmission Service at 760 Dayton Street, across from Lowry Air Base. He also continued teaching evening auto mechanics at Opportunity School for the next three years.

Being self-employed brought its own set of challenges and rewards. "You have to set goals. Without goals, you have nothing to reach for. With goals, you keep knowing what to do. My goal was to gross $3,000 in sales the first month. The first month of sales was over $5,000," he says, sitting in the break room of his shop, the rhythms of power tools grinding in the background and the occasional high-pitched car alarm piercing the ears. He proudly reports his business grossed over $50,000 in its first year. Within two months, his one-man shop expanded to include two full-time workers.

The operation prospered. "A lot of companies have fancy business plans. They write out their stuff, but the business still fails. The best plan is to come to work, show up every day, be on time, work hard. If you are about something that is good, people will follow," he states, sporting a black T-shirt imprinted with "Gooch's Transmission Service, Aurora, Colorado."

This business plan worked, and Myron successfully grew the company. In 1997, at the same location, he built a 3,400-square-foot shop with six car stalls. Three task-oriented technicians and a shop manager efficiently navigate in this hectic environment, where the smell of industrial grease and the sounds of clanging wrenches abound. The twenty-three parking spaces, filled with an array of most every model, make, and color of car, truck, van, and sports utility vehicle, reflect the company's ongoing success.

"Our business comes through word of mouth. We are too busy to advertise, and we stay busy twelve months a year," Myron states. The thriving company repairs approximately fifteen transmissions per week and grosses about $50,000 per month.

Reflecting Upon Accomplishments

Born in 1936, Myron is approaching retirement age but has no intention of hanging it up. He has turned over the daily operations to a manager but still reports to work most days to oversee the business. He enjoys a more flexible schedule that allows him to visit his five children and seven grandchildren scattered in Texas, Pennsylvania, California, and Colorado. It also affords him more time to pursue his hobbies, including attending auto shows to shop for his "dream machine"—a new Mercedes sports car—and preparing his succulent barbecued beef brisket for family and friends.

Although he is modest, Myron beams about his accomplishments. However, he quickly points out that success comes only through hard work. "Success is desire. You can accomplish anything. It takes hard work. It might be tough, but you can get there. You can do anything when you set your mind to it."

Class Acts

With a strong work ethic and solid training from Emily Griffith Opportunity School, Myron Gooch climbed behind the wheel and never looked back.

***

Author's Note: When Myron taught at Opportunity School, colleagues called him "Gucci." How appropriate because he has style, class, and an understated inner beauty. One of my first interviews for this book was with Myron. I was nervous and unsure of what I was doing. His warmth and humor gave me a much-needed boost of confidence. In June 2003, the school recognized him as its outstanding alumnus.

PHYLLIS CANO
Poster Child for Welfare to Work

"Opportunity School is a wonderful, wonderful educational opportunity for people who don't fit into the regular educational system."

Not many people can say they have turned down a personal invitation from the president of the United States. Nor can many say they have received two invitations from a U.S. president and another from a first lady. Phyllis Cano can.

A self-described poster child for the Small Business Administration (SBA), the Colorado Enterprise Foundation, and Mi Casa Women's Resource Center, Phyllis was showcased by these agencies and by President Bill Clinton as a welfare-to-work success story. And, although Emily Griffith Opportunity School has never cashed in its "bragging rights" to Phyllis's success, the school is certainly entitled to do so.

Phyllis's road to success had its share of obstacles. She dropped out of high school at sixteen to marry and was the mother of two by the time she turned eighteen. Her early choices were in sync with those of her peers. "At the time I got married and had babies at age sixteen, it didn't seem odd. It was so common. Just like smoking cigarettes," says Phyllis in a calm, smooth voice sprinkled with a Spanish twist. A middle-aged Hispanic woman with a warm smile, round face, and smooth, wrinkle-free skin, Phyllis conveys the impression she has never experienced a worry in the world, although reality is quite the opposite. Her long, dark-brown hair rests loosely on the back of her neck, and a white industrial apron envelops her short, rounded body.

When her marriage soured over thirty years ago and Phyllis was abandoned with one child and another on the way, she knew she needed help. "I wanted to do better than welfare, to give them a better life," she says. "I decided to go back to school and work at something where I could have a decent income."

An Early Interest in Cake Decorating

Phyllis was born in 1954 and grew up in northwest Denver. As a little girl, she journeyed once a month with her mother and sisters downtown to Woolworth's—an outing Phyllis anticipated with delight. The large dime store, with greasy smells seeping from the lunch counter grills and the sounds of profits ringing from its cash registers, fascinated Phyllis. But what most intrigued her were the store's cake decorators. Each time she visited, she watched them work and was captivated by the skillful way they twisted and turned their pastry bags filled with frosting to transform ordinary cakes into works of art. Her big brown eyes widened as the cakes came alive with colorful mounds of roses, leaves, and lattices. From then on, Phyllis dreamed of becoming a cake decorator.

Years later, when her social services worker helped her devise a plan for self-sufficiency, a cake decorating career naturally popped into

Phyllis's head. To make it happen, Phyllis, seventeen years old and pregnant with her second child, enrolled in the Emily Griffith Opportunity School cake decorating program in 1970. She attended weekly for a year, mastering the intricate art that had inspired her as a child. Unlike many who worked on their skills only during class, Phyllis practiced diligently at home, baking and decorating cakes for family and friends.

When her class visited the King Soopers central bakery to see an army of cake decorators in action, Phyllis eyeballed a job there, knowing the salary and benefits were decent. When she graduated from Emily Griffith in 1971, she applied at the grocery chain but was rejected because she lacked experience. Her hoped-for career took a disappointing detour. Still, she persevered, continuing at Opportunity School to obtain her GED.

Over subsequent years, Phyllis zigzagged from situation to situation, hoping to find stability in her life. She earned an associate's degree in psychology from a community college, experienced another failed marriage, trained in mechanical drafting, and worked for the telephone company, only to lose that job because of the phone monopoly breakup.

Throughout it all, Phyllis made and decorated cakes out of her home. Reflecting on that period, she says, "I had invested in the books and equipment and would decorate cakes for friends and family…I did wedding, birthday, anniversary, any occasion cakes…When I was on welfare, getting only $200 a month, making a cake here or there for $10 or $20 was good…It was a good second income to stretch things, especially in between my 'situations.' It was my safety net."

Starting a Business

Phyllis bounced back from her job loss at the phone company to land employment at Cakes by Karen. Working there planted the idea of starting her own cake-decorating business. She approached banks for a start-up loan, but they told her she needed a business plan.

Feeling dismissed and discouraged, Phyllis committed herself to writing an impressive plan that would enlist support for her idea. In 1989, she approached Mi Casa Resource Center for Women and the Small Business Administration, but neither organization had resources to help.

Ever resilient, Phyllis took matters into her own hands. "I saved $5,000 by working and doing cakes on the side. I started writing a business plan. It took me a year—that's how much research I did. I did it all by myself, did my research at the library."

Within a year's time, welfare reform had become a national priority, and issues around social services assistance exploded. Much to Phyllis's delight, resources became available. For once in her life, she was at the right place at the right time.

Mi Casa had received a grant to aid low-income minority women in starting their own businesses. Their staff reviewed Phyllis's business plan, helped her polish it, and then ushered her to the Colorado Enterprise Fund, where she received a loan that matched her own hard-earned $5,000. Phyllis states, "I started my business in 1991 with a measly $10,000."

Starting a business involves a web of intertwined decisions, not the least of which is naming it. Phyllis liked Pretty Cakes, because its lovely ring bore her initials. Her business advisers tried to discourage her on the name choice, explaining that a business name should start with a letter close to the beginning of the alphabet, making it easier for prospective customers to find it in the Yellow Pages. Potential customers, they assumed, would not thumb all the way to the Ps before randomly making a selection. Phyllis held firm, however, and customers found her. She has never regretted her decision.

Phyllis found a storefront for Pretty Cakes at 5211 Pecos Street in north Denver. To her delight and relief, her loyal customers from the previous twenty years followed her to the commercial location. "I already had all those customers," says Phyllis, her face reflecting subdued pride as she sits behind the counter in her bakery. "If I would have started at zero, it would have been harder to survive." The faint, sweet smell of freshly baked cakes permeates the air. Cakes, adorned with decorative designs, surround her.

Survive she did, barely. While her business began to thrive, her home life started to unravel. She had remarried in the 1980s and given birth to her third daughter. Her husband, however, envied her success. "He began to feel intimidated by my business. We separated. I almost lost the business and my home." As she had done so often before, Phyllis persevered, managing to dance between bill collectors. "It was real rough, but I hung in there."

Phyllis's friendly, approachable, and unassuming manner attracted customers. Her community college major in psychology didn't hurt, either. She liked people, and people liked her.

Success, Awards, and a Teaching Job

Phyllis has experienced her share of peaks and potholes, yet she embraces an enviable philosophy of life. "I am very thankful. My daughters turned out beautifully. I've had some bad times, but how can you appreciate the good times without some bad? I'm not wealthy, but I'm happy. You can't have it all. Money…started out an issue because I didn't have it. But now it is so secondary. What good is a lot of money if you are miserable? I'll settle for surviving and being happy."

Now, after many years in business, Phyllis has received numerous awards including SBA Welfare to Work, Entrepreneur of the Year Award, and Mi Casa Business of the Year. Her bakery wall sports photos of her with Bill Clinton, Hillary Clinton, Barbara Bush, and Federico Peña. She was featured in a 1996 *Family Circle* article about women transitioning off welfare. Also in 1996, she joined President Clinton and eighteen other women for a discussion on issues facing working women. She impressed Clinton so much he invited her to join him as his honored guest on a campaign stop at Red Rocks Amphitheater later that year. She regretfully declined because of business obligations. Phyllis also met with Hilary Clinton, who invited her to appear in a film produced for China's International Women's Conference.

While some might gloat over the awards received and the interactions with high-level people, Phyllis appreciates the honors but says they are not her greatest rewards. Instead, one of her most satisfying rewards is having her daughter, Antoinette, join her in the business. Phyllis jokingly suggests this happened because she was pregnant with Antoinette when she first attended cake-decorating classes at Emily Griffith, and so, by osmosis, Antoinette has absorbed the business in her blood.

Phyllis's other great achievement was an invitation to teach at Emily Griffith, an institution she dearly loves. When her niece enrolled in the school's cake-decorating class and bragged that her Aunt Phyllis had graduated from the program and started her own business, the instructor was intrigued. Her niece suggested school officials ask Phyllis to present a class demonstration. They did, and Phyllis agreed. Unbeknownst to her, Emily Griffith representatives were evaluating her potential for teaching. Phyllis wowed them. As a result, she was offered a part-time job for which she hadn't even applied.

"Opportunity School is a wonderful, wonderful educational opportunity for people who don't fit into the regular educational system," she says. "They offer training that is affordable...They offer education for jobs you can get soon. Instead of waiting four or six years, you can get a certificate in nine months...I would not be where I am today without Opportunity School."

The school that gave Phyllis the initial skills to earn a living invested its confidence in her to teach those skills to others. "It is so exciting because I am a teacher and I would never have imagined going full circle like that, never in my life...The teaching assignment at Emily Griffith is overwhelming. I get paid well. It has allowed me to enjoy my life more, like taking trips to Puerto Vallarta and Spain."

Phyllis Cano

For Phyllis Cano, teaching at Emily Griffith Opportunity School is more than a part-time job. It is the icing on the cake.

Author's Note: Phyllis joined EGOS two years before I retired, but I barely knew her. Little did I know until the interview how much I had missed. Although she could have been bitter because of all the hard knocks sent her way, Phyllis is a warm, gentle person who has grown as a result of her life experiences. She readily shares her pearls of wisdom, hoping others will benefit.

ISAAC S. POPE
High School Dropout, Pediatrician

"We helped each other. Everyone was very encouraging."

"I was so glad to see it was still there!" Isaac S. Pope, MD, exclaimed when he realized Emily Griffith Opportunity School, an institution he attended some forty years ago, was in its same downtown Denver location. Isaac, now a pediatrician in Washington State, had returned to Denver one fall day in 2003 to attend a friend's wedding. After he and his wife checked into a hotel, they immediately searched the phone book for a listing for Emily Griffith. Delighted to see it was still there, he planned a visit to the school so deeply entrenched in his memories.

Pope left EGOS in 1959, after earning a high school diploma at age twenty, and never looked back. His time at the school served as an important first chapter in his quest toward the attainment of a medical degree and a lifetime of compassionate giving.

In the pursuit of his lifelong goals, Isaac Pope would continually be forced to confront and overcome the overriding obstacle of his era: he was black. The segregated South defined his world in black and white. He wanted to experience it in Technicolor. Growing up in southeast Tennessee, Isaac had churned over the injustices surrounding him. He was bright, articulate, and outspoken, characteristics that in the 1950s could get a young black man killed for no justifiable reason. His parents feared for his life. With their blessings, he dropped out of school at sixteen and joined the air force.

Military Service and Opportunity School

Although the military would be an important launching point to Isaac's future, his first encounter proved to yield more of the same inequities he had experienced in civilian life. "When I joined the air force, the new recruits were taken to Knoxville for paperwork and physicals. The van pulled us up to a nice hotel, and the driver said, 'Everyone out but Pope.' I was the only black guy. All the others went into the hotel. I was driven across town to stay with a black lady at her house," says Isaac, with no hint of bitterness.

A huge man, Isaac is a gentle giant. His tall body, neither overweight nor thin, spills over the elevated bar stool on which he sits. He looks like the Jolly Green Giant sitting on Barbie Doll furniture.

Now reflecting on his past, Isaac realizes the importance of the military in his lifelong journey. After oversea assignments, the young enlistee landed at Lowry Air Base in Denver. There he met a woman who would become one of the most pivotal people in his life, Mary Kirk Wilson. Wilson, who was in charge of education at the base, immediately recognized Isaac's potential. She encouraged him to work on a high school diploma and suggested Emily Griffith Opportunity School, a downtown Denver institution that included a high school program.

"I ignored her," Isaac says, laughing, as he runs his hand through his black hair, sprinkled with gray. His laughter is deep, hearty, and contagious.

Wilson, who took a special interest in "her boys," nagged Isaac with the same persistence as a loving mother. Eventually, he relented. She even did some background work with his commanding officer, so when the young airman approached his superior to rearrange his schedule to attend school, it happened easily.

Isaac rode the bus daily from Lowry to downtown, attended school from 9:00 a.m. to 3:00 p.m., and worked nights at the base, studying while at work. He liked the school. Isaac felt encouraged by the diversity of his classmates, a heterogeneous mix of ages and races. His youngest colleague was thirteen; the oldest, sixty-eight. All sought the same goal: a high school diploma.

"I was really impressed. We helped each other. Everyone was very encouraging," says Isaac, who had finally found an institution free of discrimination. Everyone at Emily Griffith was on the same playing field.

While the environment felt refreshingly supportive, Isaac found the schoolwork taxing. It was not one easy A after another, and Isaac admits it was difficult at first. "I had to get into the routine. I had to learn to study again. But I liked all the subjects, especially science."

He attended Emily Griffith for a year, earning his diploma in 1959. When he graduated, he also exited the military.

Ever since Isaac was a young child, he had wanted to be a doctor. However, growing up in a family with four siblings, five cousins, and a grandmother all supported by his mother and father, his dream of medical school seemed out-of-reach. Nonetheless, if Isaac Pope was anything, he was determined.

Help from an Angel, Advice from a Co-worker

While in the military, Isaac had displayed impressive talent in basketball and football. Others took note of his skills, and he earned college athletic scholarships. But he didn't go to school right away.

Shortly after his discharge in December, Isaac went to see his oldest sister, who lived in Montclair, New Jersey. There he searched for a job. As at Lowry, he found another guardian angel to help him. Unemployed and unable to stay with his sister because of her landlord's restrictions, Isaac knocked at a house advertising for roomers. A friendly black lady answered, and they talked at length. This angel in disguise made an incredible offer. She told Isaac he could stay with her for two weeks while he hunted for work, and she would also give him one meal per day. If, at the end of that time, he had not found a job, she asked only that he leave. He would owe her nothing.

Buoyed by her kindness and generosity, Isaac beat the pavement daily seeking employment. He faced one rejection after another and was precariously close to the end of his temporary host's offer. One day, while sitting on her step, he gazed across the horizon at a huge brick building, the Department of Public Works. He realized he had not yet explored its opportunities, so he went there the next day. After waiting eight hours for an interview, Isaac respectfully told the receptionist it had been very rude to keep him waiting that long, and he deserved better treatment. Isaac's assertiveness impressed the boss, who surprisingly, turned out to be black. Isaac was hired on the spot.

Starting at $4 an hour as a sanitation engineer—a fancy name for a garbage hauler—Isaac saw his salary jump to $9 an hour by the end of the first month, impressive pay in 1960. Since he had keyboarding skills, Isaac also worked a partial second shift typing documents, all the while boarding with the woman across town.

That summer, Isaac told his superiors he planned to go to college. Recognizing a good worker when they saw one, they tried to convince him to stay by giving him another hefty pay raise. A co-worker intervened. He invited Isaac for dinner and offered this wisdom, "My advice is just that: advice. You have a lot of ability. Go to college."

College Years and the Peace Corps

These words encouraged Isaac to continue his education. He cashed in his athletic scholarships, returned to Colorado, and attended Pueblo Community College, where he played sports. In this new setting, he still encountered two troublesome barriers: lack of money and racial prejudice. Yet initiative and determination would fuel his drive. Out of cash, he could no longer afford the college dorm, but he had no place to go. He called his old friend, Mary Kirk Wilson, in Denver. She advised him to find a residence and said she would round up the money to support him.

In spite of the civil rights movement of the early 1960s, racial prejudices still ran deep. Isaac didn't know where he could bunk. Again, when he needed help the most, help was forthcoming. He stumbled upon a benefactor, Mrs. Weddington, who looked beyond color. She had connections to Isaac's hometown, South Pittsburg, Tennessee. These links emboldened her to open her door to Isaac. He stayed at her house for the remainder of that year. Meanwhile, Mary Kirk Wilson had contacted the Denver Pilot's Club, which agreed to pay $125 per month toward his room and board until he completed his junior college work.

To supplement his income, Isaac intended to work summers at Pueblo State Hospital, where all his white buddies found employment. However, each time Isaac submitted an application, hospital officials told him they weren't hiring. Perplexed, he instinctively knew the problem ran deeper than job vacancies. Courageously, he took action. "I went to see Senator Hobbs," Isaac explains.

The Colorado state senator and his wife welcomed Isaac. They asked him over for dinner and patiently listened to his concerns. The politician diplomatically suggested Isaac return the following day to the hospital to again inquire about work. Isaac says with a big laugh, "When I walked in the next day, they said, 'Mr. Pope, we have been waiting for you. We have a job for you!'"

Scholarships and help along the way from people he had impressed continually thrust Isaac toward his long-range goal of a medical degree. In 1965, he earned his bachelor's degree from Gonzaga University, a Jesuit school in Spokane, Washington. Afterward, he joined the Peace Corps, where he met his wife, Joan, while both were in Sierra Leone, West Africa.

After completing his stint in the Peace Corps, Isaac was accepted into several eastern medical schools. However, limited finances again postponed his dream. He returned to Washington, studied for a master's in public administration at the University of Washington in Seattle, and hoped for future acceptance into medical school.

Philanthropic Pediatrician, Cancer Survivor

In time, Isaac applied at the University of Washington Medical School. When the dean asked him if he was "Zeke" Pope, Isaac answered affirmatively. To Isaac's surprise, the medical school administrator responded, "Father Tim O'Leary from Gonzaga told me if Zeke Pope ever applied for medical school to be sure to accept him." Father Tim had never mentioned this to Isaac. As it had been in Denver, Montclair, and Pueblo, Isaac continued to be blessed by people along his path.

Isaac's medical school graduation was a joyous celebration. When he walked across the stage in 1974 to claim his degree, one of the loudest cheers arose from his mentor, Mary Kirk Wilson. Although they had not seen each other since 1959, when the young soldier had left Denver, they had kept in touch. Isaac's commencement was far too important for Wilson to miss.

After medical school, Isaac eventually settled in 1979 in Chehalis, Washington, with his family, which by then included his wife, twin sons David and Stephen, and daughter Theresa. Isaac established a flourishing pediatric practice in this small town, located an hour from Portland. Over the years, Isaac has worked with thousands of children, but always the special-needs children most captured his heart.

In 1996, Isaac was diagnosed with cancer, and he sold his practice. Motivated by the many caring people who had helped him along the way, Isaac established a nonprofit organization for medically fragile kids. Since 1998, he has given his heart and soul as the volunteer pediatrician for this organization. He also serves on its foundation board. And, like Emily Griffith, who resisted having her name attached to Opportunity School, Isaac initially opposed the board's choice of naming the organization Pope's Kids Place.

Isaac Pope's life has exemplified hope, love, and charity. Never one to be easily discouraged, he has navigated around obstacles and has overcome prejudicial barriers. Through it all, he refused to become bitter. Instead, he faced one hurdle after another, gaining momentum and grace with each victory.

His return visit to Emily Griffith Opportunity School resurrected memories of a time of transformation in Isaac's life. When he stood once more inside the school that helped transform his life, he described his feeling as "surreal." The tattered old brick building, enveloping an entire downtown block, looked much like he remembered it from the 1950s. While the school had changed little, Isaac has been forever transformed, having experienced a miraculous, productive life since exiting its doors.

Author's Note: On a Thursday afternoon in 2003, I received an enthusiastic call from Marilyn Bowlds, executive director of the Emily Griffith Foundation. Knowing I was writing this book, Marilyn explained that a school alumnus, Dr. Isaac Pope, was in town for the weekend and she thought his story would make a great addition to this book. I dropped everything to drive across town to interview him. I'm glad I did!

ROBERT WALKER
Clock Maker, Businessman

"I told the guy in London I was looking for a school with a little clout. He laughed and said that Emily Griffith, as far as clock repair, is the number-one school in the world."

Robert Walker scoured the globe looking for a world-class education when it was available at his own back door. Searching for training in clock repair, Bob first called London to gain information about a world-renowned school there. When the English officials learned he was from Denver, Colorado, they told him the best clock repair school was at Emily Griffith Opportunity School in the Mile High City. Disbelieving, Bob dialed another well-known school, this time in Germany. Although language differences challenged the conversation, the Germans advised Bob that one of the best schools in the world was in his own backyard, at Emily Griffith.

As a Denver native, Bob perceived Opportunity School as an institution designed for those who couldn't make it academically. "I told the guy in London I was looking for a school with a little clout. He laughed and said that Emily Griffith, as far as clock repair, is the number-one school in the world."

And Emily Griffith was a bargain to boot. "The difference in tuition was amazing. In London, the cost was $3,600 per semester, and that did not include room and board. At Emily Griffith it was $2 per semester. I always believed you get what you pay for. In this case, it was a free lunch," says Bob enthusiastically.

Tall, trim, and muscular, Bob's appearance belies the image of someone who would be hunched over an intricate timepiece, nurturing its parts back to a systematic rhythm. He has a close-cropped beard, short hair with a receding hairline, and bright eyes that complement his upbeat personality.

Bob was born in 1949. After graduating from North High School, he tried college for a year at the University of Colorado, thinking he might become a teacher. However, he soon decided that was not for him.

Disability Fails to Thwart Born Tinkerer

Bob is a born tinkerer. Even as a child, he took toys apart to discover how they worked, before reassembling them. With this curiosity satisfied, he then played with them.

Throughout his early years, Bob dabbled in machines, built motors, and repaired motorcycles and cars. At thirteen, his curiosity blew up on him, literally. A homemade firecracker ignited in his right hand, mutilating four fingers. Bob accepted his sudden disability and moved forward with resiliency and optimism, traits that would prove to be mainstays of his life. "I've always been a survivor. You deal with it and do what you gotta do," says Bob. "Basically I lost all my fingers, but I was already left-handed."

In high school, Bob's mechanical skills and interests progressed to clock repair. As a hobby, he puttered on his friends' run-down timepieces. One of the things he most appreciated was that, unlike some mechanical work, clock repair didn't dirty his hands.

Mastering Clock Repair

By 1969, timepieces had captured Bob's attention. He decided to follow the advice of the European contacts and enrolled in the Emily Griffith Opportunity School clock and watch repair program. World-renowned instructor Archie Perkins wrote articles for the industry's trade magazine, *American Horologist,* and had an excellent reputation as a teacher. As one of sixteen clock repair students, Bob could see why the comprehensive curriculum and the challenging learning environment rivaled European schools. Perkins didn't relax his high standards to accommodate Bob's impaired hand. "I think he saw me as a challenge… He wanted to see if I could actually do it. Archie was very supportive, a really good instructor."

Bob hunkered down to master this precise trade. He attended school from 9:00 a.m. to 3:00 p.m. and worked as an apprentice at a clock shop from 4:00 to 8:00 p.m. "I got paid for the apprentice-ship and got one half-hour credit for every hour of apprenticeship that applied toward my school time." During his second year, he attended class in the mornings and worked from 1:00 to 8:00 p.m. With diligence and perseverance, he compressed four years of training into two.

Bob's disability did not thwart his success. "If you get both hands in there, you can't see what you are doing anyway. If you watch a clock maker, one hand is doing the work; the other hand is holding it down." Bob uses his dominant left hand to repair and the wrist of his right stump to anchor the clock parts. "The sense of touch is most important. I have my wrist, and I have a lot of mobility," says Bob, as he demon-strates with adept expertise.

Word of Bob's success spread. The *Denver Post* featured the one-handed clock repair student in a front-page article. Bob and Emily Griffith officials delighted in the positive publicity.

When the story ran, Bob was married and living with his in-laws in Denver. Soon an Aurora rental property, belonging to his wife's parents, became available, and Bob and his wife moved into it. To receive the free tuition, Emily Griffith students needed to be Denver residents. A local clock shop owner who resented Bob's success and the recent publicity called the school to report Bob no longer lived in Denver. School officials had no choice but to question Bob. He remembers the principal's thoughtful concern while seeking a positive solution for his young student. Finally, after much questioning, talking, and problem solving, school officials realized Bob was twenty years old and could still claim his parents' Denver home as his legal residence.

Working and Starting a Business

With his clock repair certification in hand, Bob worked for five years as repair manager at the Antique Clock Shop. While he enjoyed working here, he hoped to start his own business. In 1974, at age twenty-five, with a wife and two children, he took that huge step. "I started out with $5,000, a loan from my parents. They had set up a college fund for me that I obviously wasn't going to use." Knowing that location would be key to its success, Bob set up All Time Clock Repair on Colfax near Monaco. Most other repair places opened shop on South Broadway, but Bob thought it best to be near the large, rich homes of east Denver where the old clocks, old people, and old money resided. His vision proved fortuitous.

"Starting your own business is scary. If I knew then what I know today, I wouldn't have even attempted it. Your chances of success are almost none." Bob recalls opening his doors and twiddling his thumbs the first month. With no customers banging on the door, he called a friend who came over daily and played video football to pass the time. Fortunately, business quickly picked up, and, thanks to his skill and his savvy choice of location, he was turning a profit within months. But it didn't come easily. For the first nine years, he worked seven days a week, keeping the shop open six days and doing trade work on the seventh. To add to his income, he also contracted for others.

Over time, Bob's business grew. "I loved the customers. I loved the people." Bob also relished the challenge of working on old timepieces. "With clocks, there are so many different ways they work." And through the years his three children helped with maintenance and chores at the shop.

To repay Emily Griffith for his training, Bob supported the school over the years by serving on the clock repair advisory committee. The group consists of professionals working in the business, providing input to assure the educational program remains relevant. The school also courted him to teach. Unfortunately, a teacher's salary couldn't compare with his business earnings, so he declined the offer.

After twenty-seven years of doing the same work in the same place, Bob's enthusiasm, like an aging clock, began to wind down. He longed for a change. Ongoing eye strain and the effects of carpel tunnel syndrome made the work more difficult. In 2001, Bob sold his business to his son Chad, who had been training with him for some time.

Retreating to a Mountain Utopia

Bob and his second wife, Deb, wanted to retreat from the big-city crowds to enjoy their favorite pastimes of hunting, fishing, and camping. They bought land northwest of Cañon City and now live a simple, nearly self-sufficient life on seventy-one acres in the Colorado mountains. Living like modern-day pioneers, they built their place from "scratch." They share their acreage with seven lambs, three goats, two dogs, two cats, many tame rabbits and chickens, and a cornucopia of wildlife.

Now instead of righting the rhythms of timepieces, Bob and Deb spend their days tending to their basic needs related for food, shelter, and warmth. They weed their garden, milk goats, pick eggs, butcher animals, and preserve food they have grown. Their cozy cabin, with its log exterior, radiates heat as the fragrant scent of smoldering pine emanates from the wood-burning stove. They have decorated their home with animal pelts, trophy heads, and antique clocks. The soothing tick-tocks add more tranquility to the peaceful setting of piñon trees, snowcapped mountain peaks, and the gentle sound of the wind rustling through the trees. This out-of-the-way utopia suits them. They thrive in the solitude. Bob and Deb go to town no more than twice a month. Three times a week their mail is delivered to their mailbox nine miles away.

Having been a successful clock maker and businessman for more than a quarter century, Bob now enjoys surroundings that are worlds away from the hustle and bustle of his shop on East Colfax. Still, he converses appreciatively about his career and training. "Clock repair has always been my love. I ate, slept, and drank it. If you don't love it, you can't do it." And he reminisces about the positive impact of a school whose strong reputation had reached Europe before he learned of it in north Denver. "I hope Emily Griffith stays around, because it's a great premise. The original idea is so wonderful. It has helped so many people." Time and time again.

Author's Note: *When my husband and I drove into Bob Walker's remote place in the Colorado mountains, we noticed a sign on the gate that said,* ALMOSTA. *Bob and Deb call their hideaway Almosta Ranch. To us, it was isolated paradise. The EGOS Foundation presented the 2006 Outstanding Alumnus Award to Bob.*

JOSEPH GONZALES
Entrepreneur, Inventor

"I couldn't have done it [my work] without the training I received at Opportunity School. I've used every bit of the knowledge I've gained from that school in the real world."

Joseph Gonzales remembers walking with his parents and siblings from their home near West High School to downtown Denver to watch parades. These hikes took them past Emily Griffith Opportunity School. When he was a little tyke, Joe's older brothers boosted him up to peek inside at the airplanes in the aircraft maintenance shop. Joe's big brown eyes popped with excitement. From that moment forward, Joe knew his future. "Those airplanes made me want to go to school there. Opportunity School was etched in my mind at the age of five," Joe says in a deep, nasal voice.

Twenty-five Years of Learning at EGOS

Now, some forty years later, Joe displays an Emily Griffith transcript that spans twenty-five years of sporadic enrollment. He loves to learn and credits this desire to competent childhood teachers. "A good teacher is one that opens your mind…I'm the kind of person who always wants to learn more. School is probably something I will do the rest of my life," states Joe, who laughs easily and often. With deep brown eyes and a ready smile, he sports a neatly trimmed beard that complements his stylish hair. His face radiates a healthy glow, and while Joe is muscular and well-toned, he walks slowly, with the aid of a lightweight cane, both signs he is recovering from recent knee-replacement surgery.

Imbedded with a desire to learn, Joe has successfully completed such diverse Opportunity School courses as machining, auto mechanics, and aircraft powerplant. His transcript, displaying more Cs and Ds than As, verifies that grades are not a reliable predictor of success. And, unlike some career students, Joe has utilized the skills he gained in school to carve out a fascinating work history.

Joe's father, a factory worker who served as the liaison between the workers' union and management, wanted a better life for his five sons and one daughter. He promoted education.

Joe had known since he was five years old that he would attend Opportunity School—and two older brothers went to the school before him—so he planned ahead to complete all his high school courses, except electives, by his junior year. This enabled him to spend his last four high school semesters at Opportunity School.

At age sixteen, in his junior year, Joe studied auto mechanics. During his senior year, he enrolled in morning auto mechanics and afternoon machine shop. He crisscrossed between the adjoining shops, envisioning a future career that would utilize the skills learned in both areas. However, his machining teacher didn't approve of auto students using his equipment. One morning, he reprimanded Joe for operating the machining equipment for an auto class project. When his teacher said, "You can't do that," Joe interpreted the words to mean his project was not possible. Full of confidence, Joe knew he had the talents and knowledge to carry it out. But his teacher was trying to enforce a rule prohibiting the use of greasy auto parts on machining equipment. Due to this misunderstanding, Joe received a D in machine shop that semester, something he now laughs about.

While Joe was at Opportunity School, his future wife, Theresa, attended Central Catholic High School, a few blocks away. She and fellow classmates, wearing plaid parochial school uniforms, paraded through the Opportunity School alley in a jazzy convertible, tantalizing the boys in shop classes. Joe believes this intense flirting outside the school doors resulted in the construction of the wrought iron gates now dividing the alley.

Teenage romance did not deter Joe from his career goals. During his senior year in high school, he interned at Stuska Engineering, a few blocks from Emily Griffith on Colfax Avenue. As with many job-related training experiences, this internship evolved into full-time employment. "Harvey Stuska was tough, but he was good to me and taught me things a father would teach his son. In this job, I got into the high-tech area of building dynomometers, devices that measure an engine's torque." Joe's internship stretched into an eight-year job with Stuska.

As often happens on the road to success, a mentor appears to help pave the way. Stuska recognized Joe's potential and his love of learning. He allowed Joe to work a flexible schedule to continue classes at Opportunity School.

A serendipitous moment at Opportunity School propelled Joe forward with greater self-confidence. Donald Bybee, the Advanced Auto teacher, observed Joe working in the machining lab, redesigning auto pistons, and connecting rods from an Oldsmobile to fit a Ford. While Bybee was not Joe's teacher, he couldn't hold back his positive words about what he was seeing. So impressed with his skills, Bybee encouraged Joe to apply for a teaching job at Emily Griffith. Although Joe never followed the instructor's suggestion, he always remembered the much-needed "pat on the back."

Class Acts

One of the classes Joe completed at Opportunity School was Working for Yourself. As luck would have it, this course introduced him to a future employer, the teacher's son, who owned Advanced Composite Technology. In 1988, he took a week's vacation from his regular job and assisted in this company's development of a carbon fiber frame bike—a strong, stable, and lightweight bicycle that would be used in the 1990 Olympics. He crammed more than 100 hours of work into seven days. "Little sleep, but lots of excitement and enthusiasm. I made $1,000 in a week, a lot of money at that time. The more commas, the more zeros, the more interesting the project," Joe says with a teasing twinkle in his eyes.

Risky and Rewarding Self-Employment

Joe's active brain churned out many creative ideas. In order for him to fully develop these concepts and reap their benefits, he realized he needed to start his own business. After completing the Opportunity School entrepreneurial class, Joe courageously stepped into that risky world of self-employment. "The class gave me the fortitude to get out and try it. That was scary. No more a guarantee the paycheck is going to be there. I learned when you are in business on your own, you just got 'married.' You live and breathe it," says Joe, sitting in his southwest Denver townhome.

Starting his own business appeared particularly challenging. Joe and Theresa had married immediately after high school and had become the parents of three young daughters: Melanie, Michelle, and Melissa. Because Theresa stayed home full-time to care for the family, Joe had no safety net. His family's financial success rested solely on his broad shoulders.

He was well-armed with marketable skills from Opportunity School and a desire to succeed, so Joe flourished. In his first two years of solo work, he contracted with Advanced Composite Technology. Concentrating in the carbon fiber area, Joe developed products for pool cues, golf clubs, a bicycle for the Olympics, and radio towers for the government.

Joe guided his career into a highly focused technical, research, and development business. "You can build ten motors for $1,000 or one motor of $10,000," says Joe. He chose the latter, focusing on precision, technology, and intricate detail. "I learned never to refuse a job that comes along. I never really applied for a job. My definition of luck is preparation meeting opportunity. If you have the knowledge and skills, you can get the job."

His work linked him with many interesting people and projects, including Alan Lockheed of the Lockheed Martin Corporation. A connection with a retired army general through Lockheed got him a job building a 427 NASCAR engine for a Daytona 500 race. This project involved turbo research and development, integrating the machining and auto skills he had learned during his high school years at Emily Griffith.

Joe's work history also included maintaining a museum collection of Porsches for a prominent Colorado citizen. The business agreement mandated the owner's name remain anonymous. "I was paid extremely well, but part of the deal was that I never reveal his name. This man had his own museum of Porsches, and he wanted them all to run." Commenting on the fun nature of this project, Joe observes, "From this project, I learned when times are good, rich people are gonna play. And when times are bad, rich people are gonna play."

Designing an Innovative Drill

Over time, life continued to offer interesting challenges. In 1990, he met Otto Rivera-Botzeck, who sought Joe's assistance to further develop his design of an innovative drill. "I built the prototype. That's what a research and development person does—proves the concept. He had the idea. I proved his concept. In R&D talk, the proof of concept is where it starts. It's what takes something from paper and makes it tangible."

Joe expanded Otto's concept of a drill that allows up to five bits to be stored in an internally rotating magazine, like a revolver, and developed it into a tangible working tool. They named it Redi Drill.

No small undertaking, this project included acquiring a patent, courting investors for funding, and untangling a web of legal issues. To pull off such a business venture, Joe needed to learn about business law, public offerings, contracts, and venture capitol. Like Old Faithful, Opportunity School came through for him again. He returned there in 1990 and enrolled in another entrepreneurial class where he studied units on business law and patents.

Eventually, the innovative men behind Redi Drill sold the license agreement for their product to the company that manufactures tools for Sears. Marketed exclusively by Sears, the Redi Drill was recognized in 1999 by *Motor Trend* magazine as one of the year's ten most innovative products. While Otto maintains the patent and rights to the tool, Joe was issued a large number of stock shares for his contributions.

"We did well our first quarter. The first quarter brought in a half-million dollars…Our first shareholder meeting was great. The first 250 drills made were shipped to us, and all shareholders got a free drill. We made money. It was a great feeling."

However, Otto, Joe, and the other project collaborators were not destined to realize a quick fortune. "The money has been gobbled up in business and patent protection. It didn't go into our pockets." Tied up in legal challenges, the project has spiraled into big-time frustrations in spite of the major contract with Sears and recognition from a respected magazine.

Nonetheless, Joe remains optimistic about its potential. "I still have my stock. We still have the value of the tooling. We just outgrew our patent. We may sell the patent and everything outright to give everybody a nice return on their money. There is still a strong possibility Redi Drill will reap a good financial return."

A Slowdown Because of Health

At age forty-six, Joe was rebounding from a two-year sabbatical from work. Injuries in his young life forced him into a slower gear.

When he was seven years old, he had been run over by a car, and he still suffers after-effects from that accident. To complicate matters, in his early years, he had been a thrill seeker, tempting his luck in snow-mobiling, mountain biking, and dirt biking. "I pushed the envelope, always riding right on the edge of being out of control. All it takes is a split second of time, a little bit of speed, a little bit of fatigue, a bit of gravel." During his daredevil years, he suffered a broken arm, broken collarbone, back injuries, abrasions, bumps, and bruises. At midlife, Joe's body cried out in pain. As a result, he underwent three surgeries in twelve months and had devoted most of his recent time and energy to strengthening his physical health.

True to his nature, Joe used his downtime to spin out new concepts. Knowing how physical injuries can handicap productivity, Joe developed plans for a telescopic computer stand, one designed on a counterweight pulley system that will adjust, allowing a person to sit or stand at different heights. "I can't stay in one position too long. My back, legs, and wrists have problems…There is nothing in the market for the handicapped," states Joe, who realizes firsthand this urgent need.

Like a homing pigeon, Joe returned to Opportunity School in the 2001–2002 school year to enroll in machining, where he could learn the three-dimensional technology for upcoming projects. It is a habit that, over the years, has served him well.

"I couldn't have done it without the training I received at Opportunity School," Joe says of his successful job experiences. "I've used every bit of the knowledge I've gained from that school in the real world."

Most likely, Opportunity School classes will continue to be a part of Joe's future. "I've been taking classes there for quite some time, and I plan to return. There are more classes I plan to take…There is always something else," says Joe enthusiastically. "I have more wants and more needs and more dreams. The education I need is at Emily Griffith. Besides, my oldest dream of that private pilot's license is still there."

Class Acts

Odds are that Joe Gonzales will someday enroll in the Opportunity School pilot ground school class. And, like that five-year-old he used to be, peering through the shop windows, Joe will be bursting with enthusiasm.

***

Author's Note: I conducted two interviews with Joe. Approximately a year lapsed between them. During that time, Joe had three surgeries. When I met with him the second time, he confidently expressed he would soon be back working and inventing. The interviews with Joe were fun. He was bursting with ideas, so we often detoured on tangents, and my challenge was to bring this creative person back to the subject at hand.

EDNA MINNARD
Midlife Success, Insurance Supervisor

*"I give a lot of credit to Opportunity School. They take time
to teach people a skill whereby they can earn a living.
That was Emily's one desire: to help those people who
weren't skilled to earn a living, to teach them."*

At forty-four, Edna Minnard's life would be forever changed. Her
husband, Pete, suffered a debilitating stroke. He was only forty-
five. With the help of Emily Griffith Opportunity School,
Edna overcame many difficulties thrown her way as a result of her
husband's premature disability.

Born in 1911 to Dutch immigrants, Edna was no stranger
to tough times. The oldest of six children, she had survived two world
wars, a major depression, and early years of hard work that defy

today's child labor laws. Just as she and her husband had reached the intersection to turn onto Easy Street, his health collapsed. This would become a major turning point in her life.

"It was hard to have your husband get sick at age forty-five. You never know, my dear, when something like that happens, you don't know how you are gonna cope with it, if you are a strong enough person," says ninety-three-year-old Edna, sitting at the dining room table in her neat, southeast Denver apartment. The continuous hum of Colorado Boulevard traffic seven floors below seeps through her sliding glass balcony doors. Dutch knickknacks and accessories are scattered around her. A sturdy, strong, well-built woman, Edna speaks in a full, robust voice threaded with a slight Dutch accent. Her deep blue eyes dance with warmth. Although it is a cool February day, she wears a short-sleeved printed blouse and blue polyester slacks. White heavy-duty knit socks and black SAS cushioned shoes, with a curvy sole, envelop her feet. Her attire, like her outlook, exudes practicality.

Early Married Years

A Wisconsin native, Edna met her husband at the Dutch Reformed Church in their hometown of Sheboygan. When they married, he was twenty-one and she was twenty. Rather than being drafted into action during World War II, Pete, a machinist, was tapped for essential work, building submarine torpedoes in Manitowoc, Wisconsin, on Lake Michigan. "That winter, it was thirty below day after day, with gobs and gobs of snow. He drove back and forth with some guys...Manitowoc was fifty miles away. That winter, it was so cold, and he got so sick with a sinus infection. We doctored and doctored. With it thirty below day after day, he machining out in those torpedo tubes in that cold submarine, you can imagine how bad that was. So, finally, the doctor said, 'I would suggest you go to a higher, drier climate.'" Pete, Edna, and their two young sons packed up and relocated to Denver in 1945.

As with most people at the end of World War II, Edna and her family built their future with cautious optimism. Their Dutch frugality, efficiency, and ambition guided them as they carved out a life centered on faith, family, and work. Her husband's well-paying job as a machinist and her savvy management skills enabled them to purchase and quickly pay off their home on South Pearl Street in Denver. "My husband always earned good money. In those days, you could buy a house for $8,500—I sold it in 1991 for ninety-two grand. We bought the house in 1947 and paid for it in eight years. I was a good Dutch manager. I still am," says Edna, not boastfully, but rather with a tone of authentic, homespun wisdom. She rolls her *r*'s and *l*'s as she speaks.

Their Lives Take a Darker Turn

In 1955, their lives took an abrupt turn when Pete suffered a stroke. Hospitalized for two months, he recovered enough to return home but was unable to tend to his most basic needs. "He never spoke again, and his right side was paralyzed. He never worked again. I was home with him and got him adjusted. He was a big guy, six feet three inches. At one time, I had to bathe him, shave him, dress him. Finally, the physical therapist said, 'You've got to make that man do that himself. He's gotta learn.' I had to do a lot of pushing. He was unhappy." With the help of the therapist, Pete learned to care for himself. His fragile independence enabled Edna to confront her need to return to work.

Fortunately, Edna was able to buy some time. She and Pete had built up a nest egg that allowed her to stay at home for a while. "We always had used cars because my husband was a machinist, and he could fix them. Then after we had our home paid for, I said, 'You always wanted a new car. Why don't we take that $100 a month used as our mortgage payment and set it aside for a new car?'" They never got to live that dream. "A year before we had enough money saved, Pete had a stroke. That was the end of it. Then I had to use the money we had saved for our livelihood," says Edna, revealing a tender toughness that helped her survive.

Back to Work, Back to School

"I never dreamed I would have to go back to work," states Edna bluntly. Her job experience had been limited. She had only worked outside the home before she married and during the Depression. "I worked for wealthy people, taking care of their kids, doing domestic work." During the Depression, she and Pete struggled to support their family. "We had been married only a short time. Robert was a baby. I hired out, and Pete hired out. We tried to get whatever work we could. He shoveled snow for a couple of bucks, and I did cooking. Now you can't get someone to shovel snow for all the tea in China. I made forty-five cents per hour. Then you did most anything to earn a couple of dollars."

Her pragmatic attitude toward work served her well. In 1955, nearly twenty years after she had last worked outside the home, Edna beat the pavement to find a way to generate income for her family. She landed a job with a well-to-do family, cooking, cleaning, laundering, and caring for the children. In a few years, the burden of her home life and the sweat of physical labor took its toll. "It finally got too much for me. In those days, when you worked for wealthy people, you did windows, you did floors, you did everything. Finally, the doctor said I ought to get into something where I didn't have to use my brawn but used my brain."

Once again a doctor's recommendation would spur a life change for Edna. In 1958, she headed to Opportunity School after learning about the institution from friends. Continuing her domestic work during the day, Edna attended school on Tuesday and Thursday evenings from 7:00 to 9:00 for one year. She studied Simple Business, which included typing, filing, setting up a business letter, and other basics. "It was hard to go back to school. I was scared to death I could never learn anything more," says Edna who, ironically, admits that her sharp memory is one of her greatest assets.

Typing proved a challenge. "I first had to learn to type, and that was clunk, clunk, clunk," Edna says, demonstrating with her large hands pounding on her wooden dining table. "Then I didn't have a typewriter. Pete was sick and I lived from hand to mouth. So a group of my friends chipped together for my birthday and bought me a manual typewriter. I was determined to get into the business world. I practiced at home on the typewriter all the time. Many, many times I got very discouraged. I'd say to my teacher, 'I really should give this up. I don't think I will ever master it.'"

Her patient instructor said, "No, you will be fine. Just give yourself time. Just keep at it." Edna credits her teacher's encouragement with her perseverance. "When teachers encourage people if they're a bit timid about the whole thing, it's a great asset. That's what helped me," notes Edna with reflective appreciation.

The welcoming environment at Opportunity School also aided Edna's transition. "There were a lot of people in my class, a mixture of people, different colors and races…But the atmosphere at Opportunity School made you feel like you really were a part of it. The people were friendly, and we were all in the same boat. We were all trying to learn something. I didn't feel particularly out of place at age forty-eight because there were older people who were there. I felt I fit right in."

In September 1959, a year after starting her coursework, Edna passed her final test, received her Simple Business certificate, and was sent on her way with these parting words from the teacher: "You will never be a speed typist, but you are very accurate."

Finding Work with an Insurance Company

Exhausted from her grueling year of work, school, and the challenges of caring for her husband, Edna waited until the following spring to apply for a business job. "I was tired," she says with genuine humanness. But she regained her strength, and in May 1960, she traded in her scouring pads for file folders. Working through an employment agency, she found a job with the first business that interviewed her, C.N.A. Insurance Company.

"I was scared to death. I walked into that office, my legs shook so bad," Edna says. "I had an interview first with the head of the claims department. The interview went real well, although I was frightened. He asked me some questions why I wanted to work and how important working was. Well, I had to work, no question," Edna says, emphasizing the stark reality of her financial situation. "I told them my husband was down sick and would never work again. I needed a job. They hired me right away."

Although Edna's pay was comparable to what she had earned as a domestic, the office job provided better benefits and opportunities for advancement. Edna seized the opportunities. However, success didn't come easily. "I made some boo-boos, I will tell you that," Edna says frankly. In fact, she at first toyed with the idea of quitting. Commuting to her downtown job with a friend, she used her travel time to unload, often declaring at the end of a difficult day, "I'm quitting."

Her kind and patient friend steadily encouraged her. As Edna threatened to jump ship, her friend insisted, "You've gotta learn it. What's the matter with you? You keep saying you ask the Lord to give you wisdom, and here you talk like that."

Through such encouragement and "tough talk," Edna stuck with it. She started as a file clerk, then learned the mail room, and within six months received a pay increase. Within a couple of years, she advanced to setting up claims at the transmission desk. After three years in that position, Edna, who had worked every desk in the department, was promoted to supervisor. "I had learned the whole department. I had fourteen girls working for me. That was a headache."

Edna had developed a finely honed work ethic that served her well in the business world. "I say people should be willing to learn from the bottom up and prove themselves so they can get to a high-paying job. If your company finds out that you are trustworthy in small jobs, then you will be trustworthy in big jobs. I always learned to be honest, trustworthy...My father always taught us, 'If you do a good job, you won't have to say thank-you for your paycheck because you earned it.'"

Over her sixteen-year tenure, Edna proved herself capable and resolute. Indeed, she had earned the right to accept her paycheck from C.N.A. Insurance without the need to express appreciation.

Edna retired in 1976, a year after her husband died, and the company honored her contributions by generously celebrating with a big bash. They closed the office for two hours and showered her with praise and appreciation. The retirement cake featured a large teardrop captioned, "We're going to miss you."

Retirement Years

Retirement didn't slow down Edna. She took cake decorating classes and turned the hobby into an income-generating endeavor. She also traveled to the Netherlands, retracing the steps of her ancestors. In 1991, she sold her home and moved to her current apartment. Now she basks in the rewards of a long life that include a large family and many friends. Edna remains active in her church and conducts chapel services at a local nursing home. While enjoying the intangible benefits of old age that include more time for family, faith, and friends, Edna, true to her Dutch roots, has more difficulty cashing in her financial investments. "Being thrifty, I just can't do it. It's not a part of me. I've always had to be very careful," Edna says, describing her reluctance to spend money, particularly on herself.

While many might have enclosed themselves in a cocoon of self-pity when faced with difficulties in life, Edna sustained herself with a deep faith. "I am a very strong believer in a God who protects our lives and plans our lives. I wouldn't be where I am today if it weren't for that. I believe God has a plan in our lives, whether it is good or not so good. But as that plan unfolds, we are to be faithful." It seems that, rather than weakened by her life's tragedies, she has been strengthened by them.

Edna believes that part of God's plan was to steer her toward Emily Griffith. "I started the whole business with Opportunity School. They gave me the opportunity to learn something to be able to make a livelihood for myself. I give a lot of credit to Opportunity School. They take time to teach people a skill whereby they can earn a living. That was Emily's one desire: to help those people who weren't skilled to earn a living, to teach them. It makes me very happy to know they are still doing it."

Because of her husband's untimely stroke, Edna Minnard knows firsthand how being unable to work can jolt a family. She says with pragmatic wisdom, "If you have health and strength and wisdom to do your daily job to make a living for yourself, you ought to be thankful."

***

Author's Note: When I called Edna for an interview, I was received warmly, but she said she was booked with social activities the next two weeks, including planning and executing a Valentine's Day party. When we tentatively set a date, I said I would need to reschedule if the weather was bad. She concurred, saying she, too, disliked driving on bad roads. Even before meeting her, I knew Edna was an amazing lady. At the end of our interview, she gave me a big hug and wished me well on this project.

MILROY ALEXANDER
Immigrant, CEO

*"The school represented a door opener for me…
That really sent me on my way to a good, successful
career. I can proudly say I have been there and they
helped me. When you think of opportunity,
there are no boundaries."*

Sometimes small investments pay huge dividends. Such is the case with Milroy "Roy" Alexander. Roy grew up on the Caribbean island of Grenada, known as the Isle of Spice. He immigrated to Denver, Colorado, in 1970, expecting to enroll in college. Leaving behind his homeland, a developing British colony with 133 square miles (approximately twice the size of Washington, D.C.) was bittersweet. Roy aimed for a brighter future. His home country had a 98 percent literacy rate but faced a 15 to 20 percent unemployment rate.

The country's per capita purchasing power hovered at $4,400 in 2000, with a much lower figure at the time of Roy's departure.

"When I graduated from high school in 1968, I was eligible to teach at the junior high level, and the wage was $1,400 per year. That was considered a decent job," says the tall, trim, middle-aged man who now serves as the executive director of the Colorado Housing and Finance Authority (CHFA). Roy speaks in a deep, smooth voice with a hint of a British twist. His black hair reveals a touch of gray around the edges. He is dressed in a tailored, well-fitting suit accented with a red tie. His demeanor communicates a friendly yet businesslike professionalism.

As a child, Roy worked in his parents' dry goods store that was attached to their home. He weighed sugar, rice, and salt—products his parents had bought wholesale—into one-pound bags. Most island residents could only afford purchases in one-pound increments or less. Although he possessed a strong work ethic, Roy knew his passport to a brighter future would come through higher education.

Moving to Denver

Through the sponsorship of his great aunt who lived in Denver, Roy embarked upon a journey that launched him into a whole new world. At age twenty-one, he arrived in the Mile High City, a great distance both geographically and culturally from his home. He was armed with a high school diploma, and English was his native tongue. So he was shocked and disappointed when Metropolitan State College denied him admittance.

Roy persevered. He learned the ropes of his strange new city with the help of his cousins. He also soon discovered Emily Griffith Opportunity School. Its GED program unfolded as his ticket to the future.

"I had come 7,500 miles, and I wanted to go to college," states Roy. To realize his dreams, he enrolled in the Opportunity School program, obtained the support to prepare for the GED test, and passed the exam.

"I really needed help to get into school…Opportunity School was a major, major, major help to me. It was a major bridge to get over," explains this now highly successful man. "I was not the only person in this situation. At the time, there were a number of other foreign students here, particularly from African countries, some of whom I knew held similar degrees who needed a way to get into the door, a way to get into college."

Seated in the sleek CHFA offices located in the historic LoDo district of Denver, Roy describes how his educational career took off after receiving the GED. "I started at Metro in 1971 and graduated three and one-half years later with an accounting degree in 1974." During his time at Metro, he also completed the business machines class at Opportunity School, where he learned to operate calculating machines and typewriters, skills necessary to his accounting major.

Successful Career, Community Involvement

When Roy first came to Denver, he expected to return to his homeland. However, he soon saw unlimited opportunities in this country and scrapped his original plans. Roy then plotted the steps of his career with the accuracy, precision, and attention to detail of an accountant. "I ended up working for a big-eight accounting firm and becoming a licensed CPA. I worked as a CPA for eleven years," says the Denver resident who is married and the father of a teenage son.

In the 1980s, however, he grew bored with accounting and ventured out with two partners to launch a chocolate cookie franchise business, which he held on to for eight years. Colorado's economic slump sabotaged their success. Roy shifted gears and joined CHFA in 1988. Working as the assistant director and later director of finance, he ascended to the executive director position in 2001.

This man from humble beginnings believes in civic responsibility. A charter member of the National Association of Black Accountants,

Roy volunteered for the United Way, Mile High Child Care Association, and LMC Community Foundation, and he served on the board of directors for the Denver Metro Chamber of Commerce and was a member of the Millennial Housing Commission (created to address affordable housing issues). Currently, he shares his talents with the alumni association of Metropolitan State College, the National Council of State Housing Agencies, Northeast Denver Housing Center, and the Lowry Community Land Trust.

While he has achieved much success in this country, Roy has not forgotten his Caribbean roots. Every three years, he returns to Grenada to visit his parents, who still operate their dry goods business, and to inhale the fragrant aromas of cloves, nutmeg, and cinnamon that permeate the entire island. Although many unpaved roads provide a bumpy challenge, he relishes the fresh air and the quiet beaches, known only to the natives, far from the busy tourist spots.

As the oldest of six children and the first of five to immigrate to Denver, Roy jokingly says he water-skied from Grenada to Miami and took the train from there to the Mile High City. But when he talks about the help given to him by Emily Griffith Opportunity School, this diplomatic executive is dead serious. "The school represented a door opener for me…That really sent me on my way to a good, successful career. I can proudly say I have been there and they helped me. When you think of opportunity, there are no boundaries. It is evident of the true character of the school, the variety of opportunity it provides."

When the school won the Downtown Denver Partnership Award in 2002, Roy was ecstatic. "The school is a resource that is out there clearly available that I would recommend to anyone," he says projecting the confidence, expertise, and knowledge of one whose advice would be followed and trusted.

Fortunately the small investment of helping a young Caribbean immigrant in 1970 obtain his GED at Emily Griffith Opportunity has harvested tremendous returns for Denver and the greater Colorado community. Sometimes small investments do reap huge dividends.

***

Author's Note: *I was so impressed with Milroy Alexander's commitment to the community. He has served on many boards and generously shares his time, talent, and resources. In fact, the Emily Griffith Foundation has asked that he consider a board position when a slot opens in his schedule.*

GABRIELA BOWMAN
Immigrant, Dental Assistant, Nurse

"Emily Griffith is my second home."

Before entering the doors at Emily Griffith Opportunity School, Gabriela Bowman traveled a road that took several interesting twists and turns. An immigrant from Communist Slovenia—part of the former Yugoslavia—Gabriela and her young daughter came to the United States in 1971 on a tourist visa. She soon discovered she desperately wanted to stay.

Gabriela had sampled America and its sweet taste of freedom. She wanted more. However, the U.S. government's threatening letters outlined an all-too-soon departure date. Unless she took drastic action, she and her daughter would soon be back in Eastern Europe.

Gabriella's reasons for leaving her homeland were complex. As a teacher in Slovenia, she had grown increasingly disillusioned with her government. "I did not agree with many things. I couldn't go to church. I couldn't openly believe in God. I couldn't put up a Christmas tree. There were all kinds of rules. My life was basically controlled by the government. Besides, my daughter's father was a politician and unfortunately he met another girl whose parents were high-ranking politicians," says Gabriela in an accented, friendly voice.

Years later, telling her story from the back patio of her suburban Denver home, Gabriela exudes a demeanor that makes a stranger immediately feel like a lifelong friend. Blond, petite, and tanned, she speaks words that seep with appreciation for Emily Griffith Opportunity School. Her well-toned body reflects hours of work in her gardens, which consume the entire backyard. With more flowers than grass, her surroundings are a tapestry of colors, textures, and shapes. Lilac bushes, rose bushes, and aspen trees provide hope for a flash of color in spring, summer, and fall. Blooming white carnations emit a sweet, fresh aroma that permeates the entire yard. Under her deft care, her garden looks like an imported European plot.

Help from Bob Hope

As with her many thriving flowers and plants, Gabriela's determination to succeed in the United States was deeply rooted in the soil of her new country. Through the help of her Slovenian sponsors in Southern California, she found employment in 1971 as a domestic in comedian Bob Hope's North Hollywood home. Although the responsibilities of her job were a huge step down from those she had enjoyed as a teacher in Slovenia, she was grateful for the opportunity to earn money. Besides, she worked in a beautiful home. I thought, "These people are rich. They paid good. I was glad I could work there," Gabriela says.

Even though Gabriela knew her employer was Bob Hope, his name meant little to her. Speaking no English, she was slow to comprehend Hope's reputation and far-reaching fame.

Gabriela's work ethic quickly impressed Hope. In fact, he offered her a job as his mother-in-law's companion in Palm Springs. Unfortunately, one messy detail barricaded this employment possibility: Gabriela was not a U.S. citizen. Hope tried to help her by reaching out to President Richard Nixon. At first, things looked promising. President Nixon had agreed to sign Gabriela's immigration papers but his abrupt resignation extinguished that hope. Determined she and her four-year-old daughter would not return to Slovenia, Gabriela found herself backed into a corner and running out of time. Desperate, Gabriela was willing to do anything to guarantee a future in the United States. Although naïve, she possessed a positive, can-do attitude, an attribute that would serve her well in the country she wished to adopt as her own.

With her tourist visa about to expire, Gabriela needed a quick solution. Her sponsors suggested an unorthodox idea. They knew someone in Denver who was willing to marry Gabriela and thus cement her U.S. citizenship. She jumped at the opportunity. "This is awful, but I would have married an elephant if he was an American," she says now recalling her ticket to citizenship.

Moving to Denver, Finding Opportunity School

Gabriela moved to Denver with her daughter and married the former Slovenian, who was now a U.S. citizen. "It wasn't any kind of a relationship. It was strictly for the papers, though we had to pretend it was a valid marriage." The couple remained together only long enough to secure Gabriela's citizenship. Although Gabriela and her "husband" eventually split, they remained friends.

By 1974, Gabriela was on her own in Denver with a young child. To survive, she found work sewing down jackets. A conscientious employee, she was soon the top producer. As is true with many new immigrants to this country, Gabriela found success because she recognized opportunities and pursued them. Rather than feeling deprived by what she didn't have, Gabriela was motivated to better her situation by capitalizing on the possibilities available through abundant opportunities and her own hard work.

Always a realist, Gabriela knew a prosperous future was limited if she failed to master her new country's language. A co-worker, also a foreigner, told her about the English program at Emily Griffith Opportunity School, which was located a short distance from her work. Gabriela enrolled in English courses and learned the vocabulary of her new adopted homeland.

After conquering English, Gabriela challenged herself to improve her economic circumstances. She worked two jobs, one cleaning offices on weekends, with her daughter in tow. In time, she saved her money and bought a car.

Gabriela's perseverance paid off. In 1976, after living in the United States only five years, she had accrued enough cash for a down payment on a house.

Purchasing a home sparked her interest in interior design. To learn more about this new field, she returned to Opportunity School. "It was interesting. I have a thing for it, but you need to have capital if you want to start a business, and you need to know people. I had neither," says Gabriela.

Undaunted, Gabriela continued to focus on a more secure future. Each time she explored other options, the road always led back to Emily Griffith where tuition was free and course offerings were plentiful. In time, Gabriela decided to study dental assisting. She sailed through the yearlong program and found work with a wonderful dentist who became her father figure. Gabriela dove into her work with newfound enthusiasm. "Then I did the most stupid thing in my entire life," Gabriela says. She started dating and eventually married one of the patients. Although warned by her employer to be careful, Gabriela pursued the relationship. "I was lonely for so long, and I wanted to get ahead. I thought if I got a husband, together, we could make it better."

A Bad Decision

Instead of improving, Gabriela's life went bad almost instantly. At her husband's insistence, she quit work. Within six months of their wedding, creditors harassed Gabriela, demanding she pay her husband's overdue bills. The callers threatened to take away her house and car. Her husband lifted her veil of illusions about blindly trusting others. "I was so naïve. In America, you have to be very smart. I was a European girl, believing everybody and everything anybody said."

Abruptly, her husband moved the family to Portland, Oregon. Over the next thirteen years, Gabriela's life unraveled as one hellacious experience followed another. Her husband's life centered on booze, drugs, and women. "I went through all I could possibly take with him. I was a strong believer in the Bible. I believed I could change this man. God would be with me. It didn't work that way. He was a total mess." Finally, Gabriela filed for divorce and returned to Denver with her daughter. They stayed with Gabriela's brother, who had also emigrated from Slovenia.

Gabriela was an emotional wreck. "I was falling apart. I didn't know how to go on with my life. I didn't know what to do, maybe go back to Europe…I was so depressed."

Rebounding with the Help of Opportunity School

Yet Gabriela was not one to drown in self-pity. Reflecting on her past, she knew she held the key to her future happiness. She remembered positive times. Emily Griffith naturally popped into her head. "One day I thought, 'I'm gonna check out Emily Griffith. Emily Griffith is my second home.'"

Gabriela realized she needed a new, challenging spark in her life. She evaluated her aptitudes. Nursing rose to the top. "I thought to myself, 'I never want to get married again. I will be a nurse and help sick people for the rest of my life. I don't want to see another man in my life.'"

Gabriela enrolled in the EGOS practical nurse program and in 1990 started her grueling year of full-time training. "The courses were like boot camp. There was no outside life." Three teachers were the drill sergeants: Ruby Wang, Kathy Scheich, and Bev Karika. Students who did not measure up were pulled from the program like weeds from a garden. Yet Gabriela passionately respected her instructors. Later, she enrolled in advanced nursing courses at a community college, where her appreciation for the tough EGOS teachers intensified.

"Oh, God, by comparison the Opportunity School instructors were unbelievable. They made you study, think on your own, and problem solve. You had to use your head. I see people today graduating from college in nursing who don't know how to think critically, to make sudden decisions."

Two New Loves

To conquer the challenging practical nurse courses at EGOS, each student nurse worked with a study partner. Gabriela had much in common with her colleague, John Bowman, like her an older, non-traditional student. "The other students were kids. John's wife had died. His attitude was, 'I'm gonna be a nurse and never get married.'"

From the start, Gabriela and John felt safe with each other and immune from emotional attachments. In spite of their self-imposed barriers, over time they gravitated toward one other in a way that extended beyond their nursing curriculum.

"First, we started talking. Pretty soon we were going for walks. Then we were studying together. And pretty soon we went out on dates. I'm thinking, 'What is going on here?'...We clicked so well because we had had the same sadness in the past." Pulled together by an unexplainable force, John and Gabriela surprised themselves, more than anyone else, by marrying at semester break. "We met in August and married in January. We were both older, knew better, decided never again to get attached to anybody, and we got married. God has a sense of humor," Gabriela says, laughing.

No time for a honeymoon—or even a movie and dinner out—John and Gabriela continued to hit the books hard over the next six months. "Recreation for us was going for a brisk walk in Washington Park," Gabriela recalls. "We just studied, studied, studied."

Their dedication paid off. In the summer of 1991, they graduated together, two out of approximately thirty who started in a class of fifty-five students. Both immediately found employment in separate long-term care facilities. And both felt confident in their preparation. "Seeing LPNs coming from other colleges, we are absolutely the tops. I felt so well prepared. Nursing homes are grabbing up Emily Griffith graduates. We are treated with respect. We know how to do things. RNs fresh out of college come to me and say, 'I can't do this. I am so afraid. Would you help me?'"

Gabriela has taken to nursing like a surfer takes to waves. She says, "I do not like it. I LOVE it." She particularly enjoys her work with the elderly in nursing homes. "I love these old folks. I can relate to older people. I love listening to their stories, and they love my accent. I can even carry on conversations with an older person who is not all there."

While Gabriela's life has been abundantly full with nursing and her marriage to John, she has also seen her family roles expand, now serving as guardian for her grandson and caring for her elderly mother. As a result, she has cut back her work hours. However, that is not to say Gabriela plans to leave the nursing profession anytime soon. She says, "I will probably always work. Even after I retire, I will manage to squeeze in a couple of shifts. I love nursing so much I never want to give it up."

Coming to Denver as a desperate young immigrant, Gabriela Bowman discovered that Emily Griffith Opportunity School gave her the language skills she needed to navigate in a new world, the work skills to earn a living, and a surprising bonus that stretched beyond her wildest imagination. The school brought two loves to her life: her nursing profession and her husband, John.

"I would do anything for Emily Griffith. This is the best school. All these things I have done in my life because of Emily Griffith. I don't know what I would have done if I hadn't stumbled onto Emily Griffith."

Author's Note: *I first interviewed Gabriela's husband, John Bowman, who told me his emotional story of losing his first wife to an aneurism when she was thirty-four years old. While sitting at her side in the hospital for two grueling weeks, John observed the compassionate, caring way the skillful nurses tended to the patients and their families. Devastated, John tried to make sense of this life-changing event. He decided to pursue a career in nursing. At EGOS he completed the practical nurse program and met and married Gabriela. John eventually become a registered nurse and licensed nursing home administrator. In this latter role, he hired many EGOS graduates.*

NORM HERZ
Engineer, Inventor, Business Owner

"A lot of things you learn in college are not very useful in real life...A degree in engineering is not very applicable to the real world. I learned a lot at Emily Griffith. It was the most valuable education I had."

"Owning your own business is an opportunity to work an infinite number of hours," company CEO Norman E. Herz says, laughing, from the conference room at Spectron Engineering. Norm possesses many nuggets of knowledge related to business ownership, and his pride and sense of accomplishment far outweigh any negatives related to entrepreneurial endeavors. "The business has been interesting. It's not the destination, it's the journey," he says in a deep, calm voice.

Norm's technical research and development engineering house, Spectron Engineering, burrows strong roots to Emily Griffith Opportunity School. Three of Spectron's four principal employees trained at Emily Griffith and, over the company's twenty-two-year history, Norm consistently tapped the school to meet staffing needs.

An Interest in Building and Designing

Norm was born in 1945 in Pennsylvania. "I was always interested in being able to build things," he says, looking every bit the casual high-tech executive in a dark red polo shirt and khaki pants. Norm's sandy brown, thick, straight hair reveals touches of gray at the temples.

After graduating with a mechanical engineering degree from Bucknell University in Lewisburg, Pennsylvania, he served four years in the air force and then relocated to Colorado. He enrolled at Emily Griffith in the mid-1970s to learn machining, so he could design and build an airplane propeller he hoped to market and sell.

"A lot of things you learn in college are not very useful in real life...A degree in engineering is not very applicable to the real world. I learned a lot at Emily Griffith. It was the most valuable education I had. I'm a mechanical engineer and that is why machining is so relevant. It helped me apply some of the things I learned in engineering. The education enabled me to design things with more understanding of the result," says Norm. While his degree in mechanical engineering provided the theory on how to build things, the hands-on machining training supplied the practical education.

After three years at Emily Griffith, Norm accepted a part-time job as a machinist with a local start-up business, Spectron Instruments. He struck a deal to work half days and gain access to the machine shop on his off hours so he could continue to design the airplane propeller. As so often happens, Norm's part-time job ballooned to full-time. His duties also expanded, enabling him to use his engineering skills. Work on the propeller shifted to the back burner. Other life changes ensued as well, and in 1977 Norm married. Eventually he and his wife had two children, who are twenty-two and eighteen.

Starting Spectron Engineering

As his career evolved, Norm sought ways to fulfill his desire to build things. In 1981, he founded Spectron Engineering as a spin-off company of Spectron Instruments. He envisioned embarking upon more developmental, "chancy" technology in light measurements. Norm discusses the high-tech workings of his company—high-resolution spectroscopy, satellite imaging, and spectrum measuring systems—with the ease and comfort others display when talking about weather conditions. His ability to switch between technical jargon and friendly, witty conversation seems almost bilingual.

In a self-deprecating, lighthearted fashion, Norm plays down his company's success but readily reveals his philosophy that has contributed to its nearly quarter-of-a-century existence. "I've gone out of my way to keep the company small. When it gets too big, it's not fun anymore. Then you start getting into innumerable problems in human resources, and the federal government looks over your shoulder with more intent. I like to be just under the radar."

Over the years, Spectron's employee base has varied between four and fifteen people. "A small company is sort of like a family with all the problems, too," Norm says. However, employee loyalty runs deep. Three of the employees have worked there over twenty years, and Norm goes out of his way to retain employees and keep them happy. Because of the company's narrow, technical focus, new staff members require intensive training. Consequently, profits increase when turnover is low.

An all-purpose CEO by choice, Norm relishes rolling up his sleeves and digging in. "I want to continue to do the hands-on work because, to be honest, that's what interests me. I am a generalist. In a small company, you have to do a little bit of everything. I have to do marketing and customer interface, but that is interesting only to a certain point. I really want to understand what is going on, how the product works," he explains. He is surrounded by equipment that looks like black high-tech versions of old movie projectors, with microscope-like instruments jutting out from various angles—and he is unabashedly satisfied to be in his "element."

His complicated "gadgets" have fulfilled contracts for the military and the U.S. Bureau of Reclamation. One such invention reduced from seven days to seven seconds the amount of time it takes to conduct plumb line measurements for concrete dams. Other works pulled from the company's oven include devices to measure cockpit displays for fighter planes and an inspection system for an Australian ammunition factory. Norm easily navigates through the high-tech instruments as he enthusiastically explains their purposes. While the technical jargon is confusing, the message of his knowledge, commitment, and skill is crystal clear.

Credit to Opportunity School

Norm credits much of his business success to Emily Griffith Opportunity School, not only for the training he received but for the workers it has provided. His development manager, Forrest "Frosty" Claypool, and his production manager, John Dates, trained in the Emily Griffith machining program. Over the years, as he needed additional staff, he first called Abie Ratzlaff, his former Emily Griffith instructor, to ask if the school had potential employees waiting in the wings.

"I thought Opportunity School was great...It was not hard to get into. It wasn't expensive. Learning a trade was very satisfying. I really enjoyed the structure because it was basically self-paced. You could go as fast or as slowly as you were capable of. You didn't have somebody over your shoulder all the time. But you could get the help when you needed it. The whole idea of Opportunity School is really positive. It was truly an opportunity afforded me. I wasn't as deprived as some of the people there, but it was a heck of an opportunity."

The benefits of Emily Griffith weren't limited to the exceptional training in the machining shop. While at the school, Norm found a sense of community as well. "I used to get my hair cut there, my shoes repaired there. Definitely went to the cafeteria for breaks." He used the school's barber, shoe repair, and culinary training programs to his best advantage. And Norm appreciated his diverse classmates. "It was a real interesting group, a melting pot."

Using his abundant talents, including a sharp mind and a daring spirit, Norm intertwined knowledge and skills from a formal engineering degree with valuable practical training at Emily Griffith to create a successful company. And while his business, like the economy, has had its ups and downs, it has survived and thrived. More important, it has provided immense satisfaction to its owner. "I guess I don't go along with the adage, 'Grow your company and make it big.' Just keep it fun, keep it alive, and profitable to stay around. And as long as we have interesting stuff to play with that keeps me happy."

With work as his play, Norm Herz is a happy man.

***

Author's Note: *In the middle of my interview with Norm, I couldn't help but say, "For an engineer, you are a really fun guy." Norm came across so smart, yet down-to-earth and fun.*

Three
Technology and Tuition
1976–2005

EGOS electronics students had a jump-start on the emerging field of technology.

During the mid-to-late 1970s, EGOS sailed along on its positive reputation. However, paradigm shifts later occurred when the Denver Public Schools (DPS) withdrew financial support, and the school was forced to initiate a tuition fee for students. In addition, as technology impacted the world, it also affected how the school operated and what classes it offered. By 2002, precipitous economic declines, major cuts in state funding, and an overall decline in support for public education caused EGOS to face challenges that rivaled those it had experienced during the Depression.

The school's tuition-free policy again came into question in 1977 when DPS reconsidered imposing tuition charges. In response, an organization called The Friends of Emily formed. The group circulated petitions, wrote letters to the editor, testified to the school board, and peacefully picketed outside the Denver Public Schools administration building, ultimately successfully defeating the proposal. However, as a compromise, EGOS initiated nonresident tuition charges and a registration fee.

In spite of fighting fiscal battles, the school remained true to its philosophy of providing education for all who wished to learn. In 1976, EGOS bestowed a high school diploma on seventy-nine-year-old student Ola Gore, the oldest student on record to be so honored. Born in 1897 in South Carolina, Ola was the daughter of a man who had been a slave until the age of twelve. Working in the fields during her childhood meant that Ola's education had ended with the sixth grade. In adulthood, she moved to Denver and started working on her high school diploma at EGOS in 1973.

As did its students, the school continued to reach for and achieve impressive goals. In 1976, the aircraft training program graduated its first woman, the same year it expanded its facility by 12,000 square feet. In 1978, the school established a financial aid office and nearly 300 students accessed assistance that first year. Also in 1978, the school launched a word processing program, the only one of its kind in the state. The school offered Colorado's first data processing coop-

The automotive mechanics program received the National Institute for Automotive Service Excellence (ASE) distinction in 1990.

erative program as well. To respond to the emerging technology demands, EGOS also launched computer operations and programming courses that trained students for jobs such as computer operators, terminal operators, and information system programmers. And in 1990, the automotive mechanics program became one of three in the state to receive the prestigious National Institute for Automotive Service Excellence distinction.

Reacting to growing social needs, EGOS became Denver's primary vocational training program for the WIN (Work Incentive) initiative in 1977. During that year, the school provided intensive training, counseling, and employment services for 710 job-ready welfare clients. In 1978, EGOS expanded Parent School—an exploratory program for abusive parents who have been court-ordered to take parenting classes—to a second session. Over the years, this program grew to include day and evening classes offered at various Denver locations.

Responding to increasing concerns related to the homeless, EGOS launched Operation Opportunity Program in 1989. This joint venture with the Samaritan Shelter trained homeless individuals as certified nurse assistants. To address the problem of the feminization of poverty, the school placed more emphasis on training women in careers traditionally dominated by men. It also became a center for

The EGOS adult basic education lab was christened in 1992 as the largest of its kind in Colorado.

displaced homemakers, offered a teen parenting program to keep young mothers in school, provided women's financial information classes, and worked collaboratively with social services agencies to transition people off public assistance.

The conclusion of the Vietnam War brought more changes to EGOS. Thousands of Vietnamese refugees arrived in the United States after the communist takeover of their country in 1975. In the 1977–1978 school year, 200 Southeast Asian refugees enrolled at EGOS. Over the years, these numbers increased. In 1979, EGOS received a grant from the U.S. Office of Education for a bilingual instructional aide program to provide a crash course to train Indochinese refugees as classroom assistants.

The school's English as a Second Language program grew in other areas as well. In 1980, it received a federal grant to establish a program called Colorado Refugee English as a Second Language (CRESL) for adult learners who had fled their countries due to persecution or war. Over the years, refugee classes expanded to serve students from Southeast Asia, Eastern Europe, Africa, and the Middle East.

Physical changes came during this period as well. In 1978, a new two-story building on Glenarm Street opened to house its auto mechanics, refrigeration and major appliance repair, and machining programs.

The English as a Second Language Program received government grants to support its growing needs. The school has been awarded the Colorado Refugee English as a Second Language Grant continually since 1980.

Despite the school's many transitions, celebrations were also in order. On February 8, 1980, EGOS commemorated Emily Griffith's one-hundredth birthday with a huge party attended by students, staff, and the community. Governor Richard Lamm declared that day "Emily Griffith Day." (Some years later, school officials would learn that Emily was actually born in 1868, not 1880 as they had thought. They had based the 1980 centennial celebration on her birth date as it had erroneously been listed by Emily on her DPS employment records.) The school also celebrated its seventy-fifth anniversary in 1991. Part of the festivities included planting trees around the main building.

Major changes also occurred in Opportunity's high school program. As a result of state legislation, EGOS launched a Second Chance program in 1985. It was to provide an opportunity for seventeen- to twenty-one-year-old high school dropouts who had been out of school for at least four months to again pursue their education. The flexible, individualized learning environment enabled students to complete a high school diploma or GED. As one of five state-designated centers, EGOS immediately succeeded. The first EGOS Second Chance student completed her requirements for high school course work in February 1986. By February 1990, 488 students were enrolled in the Second Chance program and 180 were on the waiting list. In 2004, 975 students enrolled and the school awarded 89 high school diplomas and 102 GEDs.

In 1985, EGOS was designated as one of five educational centers to give a second chance to high school dropouts between the ages of 17 and 21.

The school's economic impact on the community could not be overlooked. In 1988, with nearly

400 job placements and over 5,200 job upgrades, the school pumped more than $14 million into the metro Denver economy.

In spite of EGOS's far-reaching impact, the Denver Public Schools again tried to levy tuition charges in 1987. Once again the district retreated, in part, due to strong community pressures. Ironically,

Urban experts identified EGOS as a model institution.

at the same time, four urban experts visited Denver to assess the city's assets and liabilities. EGOS was singled out as a "model institution of occupational training for financially disadvantaged adults...a resource that any community would envy."[1]

Unfortunately, the EGOS tuition-free policy was doomed to end. In 1992, the Denver Public Schools' strategic plan dictated that district resources concentrate on K–12 education. All other programs were required to become self-sufficient. From that time forward, Opportunity's relationship with DPS changed. The district no longer provided monetary funds to adult postsecondary programs but continued to provide services and facilities, at no cost, as well as financial support to EGOS's high school program. In the fall of 1993, Opportunity School began charging tuition, using the same fee schedule for all Colorado residents. Tuition costs started small but increased significantly over the next decade. For instance, in 1992, forty-five hours of instruction in Beginning Keyboarding cost $10. By 2004, this figure had skyrocketed to $180.

In 1990, when its budget tightened, EGOS formed the Emily Griffith Foundation. Current and former EGOS staff members developed guidelines for the Emily Griffith Foundation. Many of those pictured became founding members of the organization.

To respond to the growing financial needs of the students and the school, the Emily Griffith Foundation, Inc., formed as a nonprofit corporation in 1990. Its mandate was to raise money for EGOS. Starting with a $20,000 endowment, the foundation grew to a $2 million organization by 2000.

Contributions to the foundation came from a broad base of support. Ronald Yost was an unexpected donor. Yost had been a plain-looking barbershop customer at the school and had been impressed with EGOS's effectiveness. Upon his death in 2000, Yost bequeathed close to $1.5 million to the Emily Griffith Foundation, which the school used for a technology center and other building improvements.

In the 1990s, Denver's economy and population boomed. Many companies started in or relocated to the metro area, and the need for workers soared. Companies competed to participate in the school's career fairs in an effort to meet their burgeoning employment needs. As a result of the building boom, enrollment in the school's apprenticeship programs—such as building trades, plumbing, and electrical—multiplied. In 1990, apprenticeship enrollment was 1,264. A decade later, the enrollment in these programs had swelled to 6,620.

As the economy boomed, so did the field of technology. In the 1990s, classes filled with people eager to navigate the World Wide Web and maximize the use of their personal computers. New course offerings included Network Technician, Cisco, Oracle, Computer Assisted Drafting, and Manufacturing Technology.

The use of computers proliferated between 1976 and 2005 impacting school operations such as registration and record keeping, and necessitating new course offerings and changes to staff professional development programs.

To meet this growing demand, EGOS expanded its library to include the Mary Ann Parthum Computer Lab. The school's auditorium was transformed into a communication conferencing center. Its adult basic education lab was christened in 1992 as the largest of its kind in Colorado, and the Ronald Yost Technical Training Center sprouted from a dilapidated plumbing lab.

Because of the closure of Stapleton Airport, the aircraft training center found a new home. In 2003, the program relocated to Front Range Airport in Watkins, Colorado.

This workplace literacy class offered near the Denver International Airport served foreign-born students who learned the English vocabulary needed in their work environment.

While many students were developing advanced skills in technology, others continued to struggle at the opposite end of the academic spectrum, focusing on remedial skills. Consequently, adults with limited basic skills continued to flock to the school. In 1997, EGOS's testing office reported that over one-third of all prospective students

Potential students explored opportunities available at EGOS, sharing the common denominator of wishing to improve their lives through education.

assessed for entrance into vocational programs were able to read only at the sixth-grade level or below. As a result, the school beefed up tutoring and basic skills education. The foundation received funding, including a *Denver Post* Press for Literacy grant, and the school received a multiyear federal Workplace Literacy grant to deliver basic skills classes to work sites.

Terrorist activities and the burst of the economic bubble affected the school as well as the country. After the September 11, 2001, attacks, enrollment in the school's travel/reservation program plummeted, forcing the program to close. Also the number of foreign students on visas and those designated as refugees declined due to tougher immigration standards. Nonetheless, enrollment of more than 1,500 students in the English as a Second Language program remained stable because of the area's heavy Hispanic influx.

With Colorado's economy softening shortly after the arrival of the new millennium, EGOS faced major cuts in state funding. The institution suffered its worst economic impact since the Great Depression. In the 2002–2003 school year, state funding decreased by over $1 million. The school was forced to lay off more than twenty staff members, raise tuition, reduce staff hours, and close multiple programs and classes.

Because of economic challenges, EGOS student enrollment declined. In the 2002–2003 school year, enrollment was 13,700. At the conclusion of the 2004–2005 school year, the student body had decreased to 10,380.

With implementation of the same tuition charge for Denver and non-Denver residents and state-wide expansion of apprenticeship programs, an increasing number of students live outside the city of Denver. In 1990, 80 percent of EGOS students lived in Denver. In 2003, only 41 percent of its pupils resided in the city.

Between 1976 and 2005, the school responded to some of its toughest challenges since its early history. Yet EGOS proved its resiliency. Through it all, students continued to flock to its doors, sharing the common denominator of wishing to improve their lives through education. This section highlights the stories of eight remarkable individuals who attended the school between 1976 and 2005.

Note

1. "Denver's True Value," *Denver Post,* October 9, 1987, 4D.

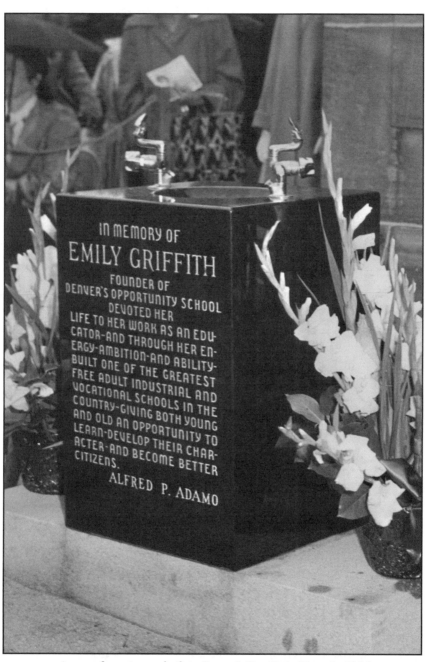

*A water fountain was built in Denver's City Civic Center in 1954
and dedicated to the memory of Emily Griffith.*

ELIZABETH COHILL
High School Dropout, Executive Director

"When you get pushed around and have an attitude like I do, you end up in prison. I got lucky...Emily Griffith gave me an opportunity. If I hadn't had something good along the road, a little opportunity to do the right thing, it would have been real easy to do the wrong thing."

Emily Griffith Opportunity School was the first school that didn't expel Elizabeth Cohill. "I think I even got kicked out of elementary school. I know I got kicked out of middle school. I was the only girl that ever got paddled in fifth grade. I was quite the little troublemaker," says Elizabeth, whose fun-loving spirit, saturated with impulsiveness and zest, speaks louder than her words.

Born in 1958 and attending school at a time when little was known about gifted, hyperactive children, Elizabeth has filled pages of her history book with negative school entanglements. By her sixteenth birthday, she had been expelled from high school for the third and final time. Elizabeth's crazy and rebellious behavior frustrated her conservative parents. Coming from educated families in the East, her folks owned a large apple orchard in Maryland and a smaller one in Michigan, where Elizabeth and her four siblings grew up. Elizabeth's well-connected grandfather threw impressive parties on the East Coast. "He called the mayors of Washington, D.C., and New York City, and Franklin Roosevelt...They were party animals," says Elizabeth, who inherited an abundant dose of her grandfather's fun gene. But the propensity for laughter and good times bypassed her parents, who focused heavily on hard work and responsibility. Consequently, they had little tolerance for Elizabeth's lighthearted, reckless behavior.

Tastefully attired in a simple black knit dress, Elizabeth tells her story, crossing her legs and kicking her left ankle while keeping the black open-toed shoe on her bare foot. Tall, athletic, and slender with a full head of long bouncy hair, Elizabeth is known as Lily to family and friends.

Early Entry into the World of Work

Elizabeth's final expulsion from school propelled her into the world of work, self-sufficiency, and independence at an early age. Her task-oriented parents would not tolerate her living at home, unemployed, and out of school. "My parents were tough. They weren't sissy parents like today."

At sixteen, Elizabeth bought a car for $50 and headed to Florida with a female friend. "I left home knowing all the big equations of life. I liken my childhood to a statistics class. It wasn't any fun, but I left there understanding money, how to make it, and you had to work hard," says Elizabeth in a full-volume voice that sounds like a hoarse Rosie O'Donnell without the Jersey accent.

"My parents freaked at my leaving. I had my little bag. My dad was standing there. I go, 'Bye, Dad! Love ya!' My dad said, 'You're never gonna be nothin' but a flunky.' It was tough, but it sunk in."

Her life in Florida was not that of a carefree beach bum. Living out of their car and showering at the beach, Elizabeth and her friend worked in a shrimp factory. Her hands tingled from daylong submersions in cold water. She reeked of fish. Standing on her feet making $2.50 per hour, with little mental stimulation, she thought of her father's parting words. "One day, I was picking those little puppies thinking, 'Wow, this sucks.'" Her father's words and the monotonous work nudged Elizabeth into realizing if she didn't go to college, her life would be one manual labor job after another.

She soon returned to Michigan. With no direction or plan, Elizabeth reconnected with her high school friends, mostly from blue-collar families who worked in car manufacturing plants. She loved her salt-of-the earth pals who enjoyed drinking, kicking up their heels, and having a good time. However, this rebellious teen also recognized being with her fun-loving peers offered more temptation than she could handle.

Moving to Colorado, Finding Opportunity School

Knowing she needed new surroundings, Elizabeth impulsively joined two friends in relocating to Colorado in 1975. This spontaneous move changed the course of her life. They settled in Boulder, sharing a two-bedroom apartment in the Lazy J Motel. Elizabeth found a job sewing ski jackets. It paid her bills but offered little satisfaction. Her father's words continued to reverberate in her ears. She did not want to be Lily High-School-Drop-Out but didn't know how to move forward. At this point, Elizabeth could have gone either way. "I was voted most likely to be incarcerated. I definitely could have gone to prison," says Elizabeth, who admits that during this period she had a few minor brushes with the law.

But rather than being tempted by the wrong forces, she found Emily Griffith Opportunity School. Motivated, yet apprehensive because of earlier school experiences, Elizabeth decided to try the institution. Since tuition was free, she risked little. She rode the bus daily from Boulder. In a school where students are treated as adults and must make a conscious decision to attend, Elizabeth thrived. She completed a preparatory class and obtained her GED in 1976.

Now, over thirty years later, Elizabeth reflects upon the school's tremendous impact on her life. "At the time, I thought the word *opportunity* was so appropriate. I really did feel it gave me the chance. I didn't want to be this little high school dropout."

Nor did she want to be imprisoned. "This whole state saved my life—Emily Griffith, Metro, my friends…When you are really powerless—and anybody who has been in poverty is—you get pushed around. When you get pushed around and have an attitude like I do, you end up in prison. I got lucky…Emily Griffith gave me an opportunity. If I hadn't had something good along the road, a little opportunity to do the right thing, it would have been real easy to do the wrong thing."

Obtaining her GED did not automatically thrust Elizabeth onto Easy Street. She continued to work at manual jobs and reside in challenging living conditions. However, the GED boosted her confidence, whetted her appetite for more success, and further ignited the desire to stamp out her father's prediction.

Starting a Nonprofit Organization

Fast forward to today. Elizabeth sits in the executive director's chair of the Association for Senior Citizens, a nonprofit organization she started in 1981 when she was twenty-two. Her inspiration for the organization came while driving to her Capitol Hill apartment. She had recently completed her degree in criminal justice at Metropolitan State College and had worked briefly in the area when she was laid off due to funding cutbacks. To support herself, she was again working in manual labor, this time in a restaurant. "That was a very low point. I never liked waitressing. I couldn't get excited about how people like their steaks."

Surrounded by the at-risk elderly in her diverse neighborhood, Elizabeth harbored a desire to help them. Flying without a safety net since she was sixteen, Elizabeth took an unprecedented plunge. "I used to see all these old people lost, struggling to survive…I kept thinking, Where do all these people go? What happens if they don't pay their rent? Why don't I help them? So I started this place." She explains further, "The whole purpose of this organization is to help low-income seniors who are having problems paying bills."

Most might expect a pie-in-the-sky organization started by a twenty-two-year-old to fail. And at first, it was shaky. Realizing she was in over her head, Elizabeth enrolled in the University of Colorado at Denver (UCD) Public Administration Graduate School and eventually earned her master's degree. Information from this program and knowledge from the school of hard knocks ushered her brainchild to success.

Located in a modest building in northwest Denver, the nonprofit has snowballed far beyond her original expectations. The association office buzzes in organized chaos as some twenty senior employees work the phones and assist clients. Its cornucopia of services includes emergency financial aid, medical equipment assistance, a housing project, and a senior job program. The office distributes more than 200 bags of food weekly and provides over 3,500 hours annually in home visits through the Friendly Visitor program. Elizabeth's adept grant writing and public relations skills have courted the support of more than sixty foundations and businesses.

If the organization's merit were measured in awards, Elizabeth's would have the mother lode. Framed congratulatory letters from President George W. Bush and many notable Colorado politicians dot a wall. Elizabeth has received such awards as the Point of Light recognition from former president George Bush Sr., *Woman's Day* magazine's Outstanding Woman Award, and Channel 7's Model Nonprofit Organization. And, probably most important, Elizabeth captured a recognition that can't be hung on the wall: She made her parents proud.

Elizabeth's success has also spilled into other areas. She started a small company that manufactures skin care products and owns an organic farm in Henderson, Colorado, where she grows herbs such as chamomile, calendula, and lavender. And, in a committed relationship for many years, Elizabeth rounded out her life by adopting a ten-year-old boy, DJ.

While serious about work, Elizabeth sprinkles life with a hearty dose of fun and excitement. She has traveled to six continents. The owner of a Harley-Davidson motorcycle, she has twice partied at the Sturgis, South Dakota, rally, and has frequently soloed across the country on her "hog." She and her brother, John, who is a year older, celebrated their fortieth birthdays by attending the world's great parties: Carnival in Rio de Janeiro; Mardi Gras in Australia; Oktoberfest in Munich; Running of the Bulls in Pamplona, Spain; Daytona Bike Week; and the New Orleans Mardi Gras.

For someone with an overactive fun gene, labeled most likely to be incarcerated, and accused of being nothing but a flunky, Elizabeth has defied all odds to use her abundant talents in a spirit of service and giving. And, in a small way, Emily Griffith Opportunity School helped ignite her success.

Reflecting on the school's impact, Elizabeth says, "I remember thinking I was really given an opportunity. I think being able to get my GED was so important. If you don't have it, there is no way you can get into college. I remember reading Emily's story. What a great story! Maybe it was my first brush with philanthropy in terms of what she did. It is a great, great school."

In fact, Elizabeth thinks so highly of the school she has even included it in her will. It's a good thing Emily Griffith Opportunity School didn't expel her.

Class Acts

***

Author's Note: *I hated for my riotous interview with Elizabeth to end. She told one hilarious story after another about herself. I wish I could have included all of them here. Underneath Elizabeth's outgoing exterior is a woman of wisdom who seemingly knows how to get the most from life and then give back.*

PATSY MAXFIELD
Business Owner

*"It is an opportunity. [EGOS] offers people a chance
to get a start... You are welcomed with open arms—
you are not intimidated. It is so accessible."*

S tudents learn about Emily Griffith Opportunity School in a variety of ways but primarily by word of mouth. When it comes to
spreading the gospel about this school, Patsy Maxfield is one of
the most vocal evangelists.

As the owner and chief administrator of the home health care
agency, Home Management Service, Patsy possesses firsthand knowledge of the many ways Emily Griffith has improved the lives of men
and women who have walked through its doors. She has both attended
Opportunity School and sent countless staff members there for

training. "I have seen staff become more motivated, more able to take control, take more initiative, be more self-reliant and more independent. I see that they can make more decisions as a result of the training," states Patsy, as she sits behind the director's desk in her southeast Denver office. Papers and regulation books are piled high around her. A *National Enquirer* peaks out from the bottom of a stack on her desk. Her office is functional, yet decorative. Family pictures, framed certificates, and knickknacks scattered throughout create a welcoming atmosphere.

Patsy's smooth, coffee-colored skin looks younger than her sixty years. Her soft, brown eyes lend vitality to her face. Tall and well built, she appears quite equipped to handle the physical challenges tossed her way in the demanding field of home care.

In the home health care industry, motivation and initiative are as essential for success as paper and pencil are in the field of education. Patsy sends her fifty staff members into private homes to care for the sick, elderly, and disabled, and she must be confident they can accomplish the job in an independent, competent manner.

Thanks to Emily Griffith Opportunity School, Patsy can rest assured. Its home health aide program has trained Patsy and many of her staff in the key areas of communicating with the elderly, patient transfers, nutrition and food preparation, personal care, and nursing skills.

Ignoring the "Poor Me" Mentality

Hard work and challenges paved Patsy's road to her current career path. Born in 1942 in Texas, she married at eighteen and tagged along with her soldier husband for ten years to his various military assignments. In 1971, after a decade of marriage, Patsy divorced her husband. She had two children by then and was pregnant with her third. Never one to wallow in self-pity or embrace the "poor me" mentality, she rolled up her sleeves, stood tall, and declared, "I am going to make a good life for us."

At the time of her divorce, Patsy relocated to Denver to be near her parents. After the birth of her third child, a son, she started beating the pavement for work. "I thought about going into nursing or social work. I needed to work as soon as I could. I wanted to take care of my family," states Patsy in a clear, staccato voice that carries a residue of Texan twang. Although unsure of a career path, Patsy's internal compass was, nonetheless, solidly pointed toward success.

Through the Denver Department of Social Services (DDSS), Patsy learned about and trained in a homemaker program that assisted people with daily living activities such as grocery shopping, cleaning, transportation, and bathing—enabling them to remain in their homes. With her training completed, the social services agency offered Patsy a job. She loved her work, excelled at it, and became a supervisor in short order.

Patsy's life floated along in a positive direction. Ever striving for a better future, she set her sights on higher goals and studied social work at college two nights a week. At work, she continued to take advantage of professional growth opportunities to develop her leadership skills. She even found time for a social life. In fact, Patsy met her second husband, Ray, at a dance. When Ray asked her for a date, she wondered how she would manage to fit one more event into her already packed schedule. She found a way, and over time their hearts meshed. They married in 1974.

A Job Loss, A New Beginning

In 1981, DDSS pulled the rug out from under Patsy by eliminating the homemaker program. Although the agency offered her a supervisory position in child welfare, Patsy declined. Her first love was home care and she remained loyal to it.

True to her nature, Patsy Maxfield did not give up. This indomitable woman has churned along in life like a '58 Chevy: durable, well built, and with a touch of class. As she encounters bumps in the road, she negotiates them with finesse, maneuvering around them with the least amount of disruption. Her smooth engine seldom sputters because she maintains a calm, even perspective. Her drive is fueled by a positive, can-do attitude, a strong work ethic, and a sense of humor.

Suspended awkwardly without a job or definite plan for the future, Patsy discussed her predicament with her husband. Ray encouraged her to start a home health business and even nudged her into remembering she had training to do this. "When I was a supervisor, they had a six-week program to teach us how to operate a home agency. They gave us a manual on how to set up an agency. I threw my manual in a drawer."

When Patsy exited her job at the social services agency, she had left the manual behind. She soon realized she needed to get her hands on that resource, even if the task seemed like looking for a needle in a haystack. She called the agency and begged to be allowed to search for her old desk. With their permission, she rummaged through a storage room of abandoned desks until she found hers. She felt relief and gratitude to discover the valued resource in the exact drawer where she had left it.

The manual proved to be a treasured blueprint for launching a home health agency. Starting small, Patsy first operated her business out of her home, employing two other displaced social service workers. Teetering between her need to survive and her ambition to excel, Patsy tapped into a client base of over 500 low-income individuals whose services had been dropped when the county eliminated its program. While many other agencies shunned these clients because of the low reimbursement rate, Patsy saw an opportunity. She knew she could turn adversity into advantage for both herself and her potential clients.

As the client base for Patsy's new agency's swelled, so did its need for staff. People traipsed in and out of Patsy's home, driving her husband crazy. "You gotta get the business out of this house!" he announced one day. Soon after, Patsy rented office space.

Growing a Business with Opportunity's Help

As she hired workers to meet the needs of her growing business, Patsy discovered many were eager to work but lacked training. To solve that problem, she turned to Emily Griffith Opportunity School. She and her thirty staff members trekked down to the school to participate in its home health aide program. Patsy paid her employees' class fees without question. Later, she evaluated the cash outlay as one of her best business investments. The training boosted the confidence and skill levels of her workers to new heights. Certain of its efficacy, Patsy has sent countless others to the school for training over the years.

As her business grew, so did Patsy's accomplishments. In 1984, she added another credential to her name. Her slow, steady accumulation of college credits resulted in a bachelor's degree in social work from Metropolitan State College.

With her undergraduate degree completed and more free time on her hands, Patsy volunteered at the school that had been so instrumental in her success. She served on Emily Griffith's Home Health Aide Advisory Committee, which provided input on curriculum and program delivery. As chair of the committee for several years, she even testified before the Denver Public Schools Board of Education about the valuable contributions Opportunity School makes to the community.

When Patsy speaks about Emily Griffith, her words come straight from the heart. "It is an opportunity. It offers people a chance to get a start. It's a place where you go to feel you belong. You are welcomed with open arms—you are not intimidated. It is so accessible. It's okay for everybody to go there…There isn't one person more acceptable than another."

To this day, Patsy continues to send staff to the school for training. Commenting about her most recent referral, she notes, "I could see a change in her. She was scared and afraid to do anything. Now after the class and passing the certification test, she has grown so much."

Although approaching retirement age, Patsy has no intention of hanging it up. Her love for her work shines through as she relates how her agency helps homebound clients. "I like my job because I am filling a need. You can do a job for money or for benefiting others. I have made good money, although it was up and down as it was getting established...I get my satisfaction in working with people. When it all boils down, people get sick in the same way and they all need the same type of help."

While retirement is not on her horizon, Patsy takes more time these days for her family, which has expanded to include two stepchildren and six grandchildren. "I was determined to do well for my kids, and they all turned out well and went to college," says Patsy.

She also makes more time for fun. Patsy occasionally trims her work schedule to join her husband for long weekend escapes. A graduate of the Emily Griffith aircraft training program, Ray works as an aircraft technician for Continental Airlines. His flight privileges enable them to travel at hardly any cost.

In reflecting on her business success, Patsy credits Emily Griffith Opportunity School with helping her along the way. In thanks, she gives back to the school by serving as one of its loudest crusaders, spreading the good word about its wonderful programs. May this messenger never be silenced!

<hr />

Author's Note: I knew Patsy when I worked at EGOS and she served on the Home Health Aide Advisory Committee. In fact, we worked together on her presentation to the DPS Board of Education. I hadn't seen her for several years when I ran into her one day at the supermarket. I told her about my book project, and she agreed to an interview.

HAI TRAN
Prisoner of War, Barber

"I liked the school very much. It was my first school in the United States...I was from a poor country. It seemed wonderful."

Hai Tran measures happiness with a shortened yardstick. Opportunity and freedom, precious gifts he has not always had, are its markers.

A native of Vietnam, he endured three years as a prisoner of the Vietcong after his country's civil war ended in 1975. Hai had soldiered for the losing side. The communists' philosophy, the losers must suffer, forced him to exist in the prison camp's nightmarish landscape, blistering in the pain of hard labor, hunger, and brutal political lessons. Although a young man with his life fully ahead of him, he harbored few hopeful thoughts of the future.

Now living in Denver, Colorado, where the air is crisp and dry and the days provide a sampling of all four seasons, Hai is several thousand miles from his tropical homeland. However, the changes that have occurred in his life over the past three decades extend beyond geographic. They are political and personal. Although his past is peppered with pain and suffering, his personality radiates joyful exuberance. And Emily Griffith Opportunity School played an important role in Hai's adjustment to his new homeland halfway around the world.

Hai was born in 1939. A small man, he operates in fast-forward. His thin body appears one missed meal away from starvation. A cell phone attached to the loop of his tan denim trousers looks as if it could effortlessly pull the pants to his knees. Hai's full head of dark hair shows no sign of gray. Two deep lines crease his forehead, three short crevices radiate from the corner of each eye, and a dark neatly trimmed mustache shadows his upper lip.

The War and Its Bitter Aftermath as a POW

At the outbreak of the Vietnamese civil war in 1945, Hai lived with his mother and siblings in a poor country village. His older sister, who had married a doctor and lived in Saigon, moved her mother and siblings to the city where it was safer. After completing French high school and training as an architect, Hai was drafted in 1968 as an officer into South Vietnam's army. He worked as a linguist teaching Vietnamese to Korean and American soldiers, simultaneously learning bits and pieces of English. "I began to learn English on my own. I listened to tapes. It was hard," says Hai in a high- pitched, youthful, jittery voice.

With the war's bitter end in 1975, Hai became a prisoner of the communists, eking out an existence on a diet of rice and vegetables boiled in water. His captors attempted to "reeducate" the prisoners on the virtues of communism. Although he lived in deplorable conditions, Hai found two joys in the camp. One was a pet duck that provided love, nurturing, and a daily egg that gave him the sustenance he needed to survive. The second was cutting his fellow prisoners' hair. "I learned barbering by myself. I cut hair often," says Hai proudly.

In 1978, the communists released Hai from the concentration camp, and he returned to war-torn Saigon, exhausted but joyful. It was bittersweet. He had been freed from the bondage of prison into a life bound by the dictates of the communist regime. He felt like a bird set free from a cage only to discover its clipped wings prevented it from flying. To further complicate matters, his mother had died and most of his siblings, nieces, and nephews had gotten out before the communist takeover and had immigrated to the United States and Canada. However, the good news for Hai was that his skills as an architect technician were in demand. He immediately found work with the City of Saigon. Also, in 1980 at age forty-one, he married, and within two years his wife gave birth to two sons.

It was not long before Hai decided he wanted a better life for his spouse and two young boys. In 1982, he applied to immigrate to the United States. With this request, the Vietnamese government forced Hai to relinquish his employment. Consent to leave came slowly. Although he received a passport, the communist government waited nine grueling years to stamp its approval, deadlocking Hai and his family in limbo. "When I applied to go to the United States, I couldn't work. For nine years, I couldn't work. I lived on the support of my sister and nephew. We were very poor. When we got the approval, we were very happy."

Attending Opportunity School

When at last his request was granted, Hai and his family immediately came to Colorado. His sister, who lived in Aurora, helped in the transition. In addition to providing initial housing, she directed Hai to Emily Griffith Opportunity School, which is a magnet for the foreign-born immigrating to the Denver area. "I liked the school very much. It was my first school in the United States. It was amazing. Everything was good. It was convenient and luxurious. I was from a poor country. It seemed wonderful. The teachers and students were friendly."

Hai enrolled in English and auto mechanics. His sister thought automotive work would provide an opportunity for employment, even though Hai had never owned a car and knew little about their complicated engines. Undaunted, Hai faithfully attended classes and dedicated himself to his studies. "I was never absent an hour. I was always present. I rode the bus to school from Aurora."

Although Hai completed the yearlong course, he was unable to find work as an auto tech. "It was difficult to find a job. I don't think they [potential employers] trusted me."

Disappointments and Continued Resilience

Ever resilient, Hai planned to switch gears to study engineering. However, more obstacles interfered. Hai's wife had left him and his two young children shortly after they arrived in Denver. Eager to marry again, Hai had arranged to wed a woman twenty years his junior, who still resided in Vietnam with a sick three-year-old child. In 1994, he traveled to Vietnam and married her. Returning to the United States soon after, Hai sent his new wife support for four years while she awaited permission to join him in this country.

Hai's new family situation necessitated that he scrap his engineering plans to find work as soon as possible. Assessing his skills and situation, Hai recalled his time in the prison camp and his talent for cutting hair. In 1995, he returned to Emily Griffith to study barbering. "I was very happy and satisfied at Opportunity School. I paid only a little tuition. Opportunity School helped me get my license. Sandra Peoples was my teacher. I owe her a lot."

This time, his choice proved fruitful. He completed the program, passed his licensure test, and embarked on a career path doing what he enjoyed. "In Vietnam, barbering was a hobby. Now it is my work. I like my work. I can bring satisfaction to my customers. They appreciate my talent," says Hai with pride and a sense of accomplishment.

Success as a Barber, Joyful Optimism as a Philosophy

For the past seven years, Hai has cut hair at a barber shop in the Bear Valley Shopping Center. Working Tuesdays through Saturdays, he bikes to his job and is paid on a commission, making 70 percent of the $12 fee. He does around ten haircuts each day. "When you work, it is good for your health, for your thinking. The result of your work is to produce. I work and make people wear beautiful hair," Hai says with joyful satisfaction.

His life today is a far cry from the jungles of Vietnam. Hai lives with his two sons in a third-floor apartment in a southwest Denver low-income housing development. When he moved to the apartment eight years ago, his subsidized rent cost $21 a month. Today, financially self-sufficient, Hai pays $900 a month for the same dwelling. From his balcony, the mountains look so close and clear it seems an outstretched hand could touch them.

While Hai has found success at work, good fortune has eluded him in the marital arena. His second wife divorced him shortly after arriving in the United States. "My second wife lived with me three months. She is a runaway wife. I was poor, only a poor barber. She sent me divorce papers."

In spite of two failed marriages, Hai has made yet another attempt to find a wife. In April 2002, he returned to Vietnam and claimed his third bride. She now patiently awaits approval from the United States to join him in Denver.

If he has been in unlucky in love, Hai has hit the jackpot in child rearing. "I raised my sons. I taught them to do everything. I was the father and the mother." Hai's older son, born in 1980, graduated from high school and works full-time for the postal service. His younger son, born in 1982, graduated second in his class from Sheridan High School and has completed his master's degree in business administration from Denver University.

Hai's life is a mosaic of suffering, challenges, and victories. Still, difficulties and disappointments have failed to sour his spirits. Instead, he appears to appreciate them. "I love my past. I expect my future, like a continuation. I use my past to make my future. I cannot grow without roots," he says philosophically. "I am glad to be in America because there is a lot of opportunity and freedom. My dream is not big; it is small. I can reach it. My dream is to live without worry. Right now I have nothing to worry about. I am a happy man."

***

Author's Note: After writing his story, I met with Hai to review it for accuracy and to obtain his signature for inclusion in the book. As he read it, he became visibly frightened, concerned the communists in his home country might retaliate, even now more than thirty years later. He took the story home, discussed it with his sons, and decided to grant permission for its use. In part, his reasoning was an abiding indebtedness to Emily Griffith Opportunity School and its positive impact on his life.

SHARELLE PANKEY
Artist, Fashion Designer

"One day this guy came in and asked if I went to a design program at a fancy college. I said, 'No, I went to Emily Griffith.' He looked at me like I was crazy. I have seen people go to other prestigious schools. But they don't learn how to sew."

While most people think art should be hung on walls, Sharelle Pankey believes it should be worn. Art designed by Sharelle is worn by many people, well-known and not, throughout Denver and beyond.

Since childhood, Sharelle wanted to be a clothing designer. She would scout her sisters' closets, seeking clothes with interesting fabrics, and cut them into designer outfits for her Barbie doll. The clothes she often chose happened also to be some of her siblings' favorites. "If the shirts were new, they would be *sooo* mad at me," Sharelle says. Consequently, her mother disciplined Sharelle, but even that did not discourage this budding designer.

Love of Art

"I love art. I always felt clothes are art," explains Sharelle, who is a walking display of the design elements. Her black, floor-length skirt reveals a splash of jewel-colored flowers. She wears a turquoise, natural fiber shirt over a black scooped-neck knit shell. Her clothing colors bring out the best in her cinnamon-colored skin and flatter her full figure. Her hair, dark at the roots, sports an auburn tone that echoes the color of her smooth, healthy-looking skin.

"My mom was an artist," Sharelle says, as she adjusts her clunky bracelet made of large polished black and white stones held together by silver moldings. It is difficult to imagine Sharelle ever leaving home without a full set of accessories. Today, she also wears large black hoop earrings. The final touch to her ensemble is a splash of rose color on her full lips, a hue that also ribbons through her patterned skirt.

While Sharelle's mother was a talented artist and instilled a love of design in her six children, she was also a realist. As a single parent, she had to make a living to support her family. She gained valuable wage-earning skills in the power sewing program at Emily Griffith Opportunity School and worked as an industrial sewing operator in a Denver mattress factory. Later, Sharelle would follow her mother's footsteps by attending Opportunity School, too.

Born in 1958, Sharelle married her sweetheart, Ed, upon graduating from Denver's Thomas Jefferson High School. In the early 1980s, after giving birth to two sons and a daughter, Sharelle rekindled the creativity itch she'd indulged as a child. This time, her art materials included a sewing machine and a sketch pad.

Fascination with Sewing, Training, and Encouragement from EGOS

"Ever since I was a little girl, I was fascinated with the sewing machine," Sharelle explains. Although her mother was an excellent seamstress, she had never taught Sharelle to sew. Sharelle looked to Emily Griffith Opportunity School to fill the gap. Prompted by a desire to learn to sew as well as a longing for adult interaction, Sharelle attended weekly evening clothing construction classes offered by Opportunity School in the early '80s. Soon she was taking day classes. In time, she enrolled in the full complement of sewing and design courses including textiles, fashion sketching, and wearable art.

Without realizing it, Sharelle had embarked on the path to entrepreneurship. "In all the classes I took at Emily Griffith, the teachers promoted business. They would say, 'If you had a business, you could do this or that.'" While in Ilse Romoth's pattern drafting class, Sharelle started making hats. Romoth encouraged her students to bring their own designs for "show and tell." Reluctantly, Sharelle displayed her creations to her fellow fledgling designers. Romoth was impressed by Sharelle's work and urged her to consign her hats to stores.

Sharelle said, "No, I don't think they are good enough."

"Yes, you go put those in stores," the persistent instructor insisted. Unconvinced, Sharelle ignored her teacher's advice.

Thankfully, her teacher did not give up easily. Each week in class, Romoth asked Sharelle if she had consigned her creations. Each time, Sharelle sheepishly admitted she had not. Finally, after ongoing badgering from her instructor, Sharelle caved in. By the end of the school year, she had placed her hats in five Denver stores.

Design Trademark: The Treasure Coat

Thus was the start of Sharelle's design career. In the late 1980s, she launched her own home-based business, first making headwear. Eventually, her work evolved to wearable art in the form of painted denim jackets. While her products were popular and beautiful, she encountered an irritating and potentially costly problem: people copied her work. In addition, denim art was a crowded field.

By the 1990s, Sharelle's business had outgrown her home. She had rented a storefront for her design studio. She knew in order to stay in business and remain competitive, she needed a new product. She channeled her creative talents in a new direction. Remembering Romoth's advice to stay five steps ahead of everyone else, Sharelle designed a product with special appeal to African American women.

Sharelle created a "treasure coat," a design item that came to be her signature trademark as undeniably linked to her as the *Mona Lisa* is linked to da Vinci. She chose to name her creation the treasure coat because each garment is a unique pattern, individually designed, and different from all others. One side of the reversible coat is a woven, authentic African mud cloth. On the other side, Sharelle pieces together colorful fabrics, specially designed to reflect the wearer's personality. Created when African textiles and home furnishings were first building momentum, Sharelle's coats quickly took off, gaining an avid following of fervent buyers.

Sharelle tells her story from her design studio on busy East Colfax Avenue. She tosses a piece of scrap fabric into a wastebasket overflowing with colorful threads and material pieces as traffic sounds, including the occasional horn of a disgruntled driver, filter into the studio. Three powerful industrial machines, a serger, and a heavy-duty iron perch on various work spaces. A bright orange dinette chair rests near a sewing machine, patiently waiting for an occupant. Overhead ceiling fans buzz in an effort to circulate the hot summer air.

Sharelle explains that she works with each client to customize the colors and fabric of the coat. The flowing, colorful, kimono-style garment is "one size fits all." She says, "My clothes are art, African American folk art, like a quilt. They are wonderful, exciting...When you wear art, you feel good."

Many customers have sought out Sharelle's distinctive creation including Mrs. Harry Belafonte, Denver artist Ed Dwight, Eugenia

Bickerstaff (the wife of a former Denver Nuggets coach), and many other stylish women from New York and California. Each year, Sharelle also participates in African American art fairs across the country.

While her colorful coats have attracted high-profile buyers, Sharelle has priced the garments under $450 in an effort to make them affordable for the average person. "Everybody buys them, the whole gamut of people. My coats have been all over the world," notes Sharelle.

A Focus on Customer Service, A Passion for Wearable Art

Unlike some temperamental artists, this designer loves working with customers and aims to satisfy them. "Everybody who buys my coat either calls me or comes by and tells me a story about a reaction they had with my treasure coat. That makes me feel so good." Sharelle shares stories of patrons even getting offers from people wanting to buy the coats off their backs.

With a warm, easy smile and down-to-earth conversational style that instantly puts others at ease, Sharelle instills a sense of relationship that goes beyond business. "You know what really makes me feel good? When people say, 'My friend made this for me.'. . . Half the people I never met until they came in for a jacket. But that makes me feel good that they feel I'm their friend."

While her treasure coat has proven to be her bread-and-butter, Sharelle's fashion career has encompassed many other interesting assignments. She designed an entire scene for the television show *Diagnosis Murder* and has created clown suits, band uniforms, and unique costumes.

Abundantly endowed with artistic talent, Sharelle also recognizes she could not be where she is today without the help of others. She credits much of her success to the support of her husband and to the training at Emily Griffith. "I attribute all the things I have done to Emily Griffith. Ilse's design class was the most inspiring. She really promoted business."

Sharelle is proud of the education she has received at Opportunity School. "One day, this guy came in and asked if I went to a design program at a fancy college. I said, 'No, I went to Emily Griffith.' He looked at me like I was crazy. I have seen people go to other prestigious schools. But they don't learn how to sew. At Emily Griffith, you learn how to sew."

In any project Sharelle tackles, no matter how challenging or difficult, she knows the key is believing she can handle it. "If your brain tells you, 'You can't do it,' you can't. If you make up your mind you can do it, you can do anything."

That is not to say Sharelle believes running a design business is a piece of cake. "It takes a lot to own a business. People think it is so easy. Everything, down to the paper clips, costs money." Nonetheless, Sharelle acknowledges she has done well. Profits from her business helped pay her daughter's college education. Sharelle adds, "But I have been in business for thirteen years. When am I going to make my million?"

In spite of the financial challenges of business ownership, Sharelle is the first to admit her work is not about the paycheck. "What I do here is a passion. It's not about money. It's about doing what I love."

<hr />

Author's Note: Since my interview with Sharelle, she has moved her design studio back to her home. Sharelle has received many accolades for her outstanding talent. She was recognized by Westword *newspaper's "Best of 1997" Locally Produced Coats, featured in the fashion sections of the local papers and in a national travel magazine in 1998. Like her coats, she is a treasure!*

LAURA GEISER
Early Childhood Educator

"I learned so much [in parenting classes]...I was so inspired because I didn't have to use the kinds of treatments I had grown up with."

To say Laura Geiser felt unprepared for parenthood is a gross understatement. In 1991, with fear and trepidation, she held her new baby, the first infant she had ever cradled in her arms. "How green I was...how afraid I was of children. I did not have a clue as to what to do as a parent," says Laura. However, unlike many who sail blindly into this difficult, all-encompassing job, Laura fully recognized her deficiencies and was determined to overcome them. She turned to Emily Griffith Opportunity School, where she found assistance that not only empowered her as a parent but also pointed her toward a whole new career.

Class Acts

Early Home Problems, Moving to Denver, Starting a Family

Like many others, Laura traveled a winding path to Emily Griffith. Her journey started in 1979. At nineteen, she and a female friend left their homes on Long Island, New York, and headed west with no plan and no end destination. "We just got in the car and drove away," Laura says, with a tinge of sadness. Her rearview mirror reflected an abusive home situation that had jeopardized her physical health. "When I was growing up, my dad was a rage-aholic. He would blow up all the time about nothing in particular…He didn't have any control. He would need to rage…If you got in his way, you were victimized…always put down," says Laura in a soft, fragile voice. She is tall, thin, and youthful looking. Her bouncy brown hair, repeating the color of her button eyes, sparkles with golden highlights. Her slender legs, crossed, swivel nervously.

Laura's stress at home manifested in an eating disorder. "I really think I would have died if I had stayed there…I became very ill and couldn't eat. The doctor said it was caused by stress. I realized the only way for me to have a normal life was to move."

When Laura arrived in Denver, her money had evaporated. So, she found a job and planted roots. Within a few years, she married. She and her husband embarked on a job with a moving company that took them, via eighteen-wheeler, to all forty-eight mainland states and parts of Canada. Laura's gentle, innocent appearance belies the fact that she hung out in truck stops, climbed into elevated cabs, and conversed on a CB radio. While life on the road had its share of adventures, Laura and her husband also realized they wanted a family. The thought simultaneously paralyzed and invigorated her.

"I never wanted to have any children. I grew up in a situation I would never repeat. It was pretty insane," Laura explains. "There was domestic violence in my family…not physical…but a lot of emotional abuse." But Laura loved her husband and longed to have children with him, in spite of her difficult background. Eventually, Laura and her husband came off the road and launched a successful moving business in Denver. In 1991, when their son, Joseph, was born, Laura left the business, thinking their family life, which had become shaky, would stabilize if the lines between home and work were more separate.

Seeking Help as a Parent, Finding Support from EGOS

"I had no parenting skills. I didn't have any role models," says Laura frankly. "I didn't have any experience to base bringing a child into this world…It was very concerning to me."

Laura recognized she needed help. She learned about the wide array of parenting classes at Emily Griffith Opportunity School and enrolled in the Early Childhood Education (ECE) class taught by Aroxie Feldman off campus at Fairview Elementary School in west Denver. Emily Griffith also operated a day care center for children of its students at this location, so Joseph was enrolled in the infant classroom.

"Aroxie basically changed my life. She is very kind and encouraging. That was something from an adult I had never known." Laura's teacher became her role model.

"I learned so much. I am so thankful because I had so many problems. I was so inspired because I didn't have to use the kinds of treatments I had grown up with."

The class embraced a dual focus of strengthening parenting skills and preparing students for work in child care. Although Laura enrolled to polish her parenting skills, she also became hooked on the early childhood education field. After completing the Emily Griffith program, she transferred to Community College of Denver, eventually earning an associate's degree in early childhood education.

As her educational world expanded, Laura's home life suffered. While attending Emily Griffith, her marriage disintegrated. "When I had my child, I became overprotective. I didn't have good skills of any kind. I might have wanted things my way," states Laura in blunt self-appraisal. "My husband was probably turned off by some of the arguments we had. Compared to what I grew up with, I thought I was mild, but if you're not used to that, it is very offensive. I thought I was doing well. Little did I know I had a long way to go."

A New Career

With school completed, Laura found work at Highlands Early Learning Center, eventually becoming its director. In this role, she was responsible for twenty employees and 123 children, ages six weeks to twelve years.

In two years, Laura chalked up valuable skills as a facility administrator. Also during this period, two major events left their indelible marks on her life. She remarried, and her son, Joseph, was diagnosed with Perthes, a hereditary disease that affects the development of hip joints. Initially, the ailment caused Joseph so much pain he could not put on his shoes, socks, or pants. After the diagnosis, Joseph's legs were confined by two casts attached by a bar. Laura's training, particularly as it related to a challenged child, served her well. However, parenting a sick boy and administering a large center depleted Laura, pulling her in opposite directions. Her demanding job as a child care center director suffered. Consequently, her divided loyalties spurred her into new directions.

Purchasing a Child Care Center

One day, on a fluke, Laura thumbed through listings of child care centers for sale. Carousel Learning Center in Lakewood caught her eye. The business seemed reasonably priced, and Laura felt she had developed the skills necessary to own and operate her own center. She also envisioned having her own facility would provide flexibility to be more available to Joseph. In October 2000, using equity from their home, Laura and her husband, Bob, purchased the center.

The facility started as a tri-level brick home. When Laura purchased the property, the mortgage company described it as in need of "deferred maintenance." That meant little to Laura until she spent her first day there. "I didn't spend a lot of time here before I bought it...I was looking at it through rose-colored glasses. The first day, I just cried because the toys were so pathetic. I filled the dumpster. It all needed to be painted…It was in bad shape." Fortunately, her husband's construction skills came to the rescue. Bob not only shaped up the place, but also built new play equipment and converted the garage into an additional toddler room. "It was a partnership all the way," Laura says, describing her husband's active involvement.

Now Laura's center is enrolled to capacity, with thirty-six children ranging in age from one to six years. Her six dedicated employees keep it running smoothly. "The staff is wonderful. They're a lot like family," Laura says sitting in the toddler room on a child's chair a foot off the floor. Radiator pipes bang in the background, heating the room on a chilly January day. Three of the four walls, each painted in a different bright primary color, exude action. Pictures and words posted at toddler eye level, reach an adult's knee. Toys, diapers, and midget-size furniture fill the room.

Laura's facility is open weekdays 6:15 a.m. to 6:00 p.m., and her job demands sixty-hour workweeks, physical strength, and management savvy. She loves it because every minute is varied. Sometimes she manages infectious outbreaks of measles and the flu. She frequents the grocery store, as feeding thirty-six children two meals and a snack daily averages a cart full of food every twenty-four hours. Laura also teaches. "I work in every classroom every week. That way, I'm in touch with all the children." Because of the need to connect with parents, she is present to close the center each day so she can talk with the adults as they pick up their children.

To Laura, the most important part of her job is supporting the parents, many of whom are single and struggling. Knowing firsthand the far-reaching effects of negative parenting, Laura nurtures the moms and dads. "I thought my work would always be with the children. But it's with the parents, because if I can communicate with them and they can be happy, healthy, and have self-esteem, and know they are doing the right thing, that is going to roll off onto the children more than anything I do."

Besides the satisfaction of helping children and families, Laura loves the independence of being her own boss. "I don't have to worry about what anybody thinks about what I'm doing. I can sit down and have a cup of coffee in the kitchen. The hours don't seem long."

Owning her own business has given Laura the flexibility to zero in on her son's needs. Joseph is now a typical teenager, doing everything expected of someone his age. Physically able, he is a happy, well-adjusted boy.

"I'm really proud of Joseph...We helped him learn about self-esteem and accepting children with differences and knowing he is special...I think Joseph's success story is directly related to going to Emily Griffith."

And over the years, the negative effects of Laura's early life in a dysfunctional home have been minimized by the education she received at Emily Griffith, the love and acceptance of a nurturing husband, and a strong Christian faith. In fact, Laura's animosity toward her parents, now in their eighties, has dissolved. "My parents didn't mean to hurt me. They just didn't know any better...I love them and I forgive them, and I hope they do the same for me."

Laura Geiser, the victim of an abusive childhood, sought to break the cycle of negative parenting by enrolling at Emily Griffith Opportunity School. Not only did this early childhood training help her become a model parent, it also channeled her into a career where she daily helps and supports other parents. As a bonus, she works in a job where the hourly perks include holding and cuddling little children, something she now does with confidence and ease.

***

Author's Note: Laura Geiser speaks passionately about how Emily Griffith changed her life both personally and professionally. She expressed so much appreciation to her instructor, Aroxie Feldman, who is a master teacher and "grand dame" at the school. Aroxie is dearly loved by students and staff alike.

NISA'A AMEEN
Upholsterer, Realtor

*"The reasonable tuition got me in the door. The high-quality
education sold me and kept me coming back."*

Nisa'a Ameen knows an underrated treasure when she sees it,
whether a piece of discarded furniture, undervalued real
estate, or quality adult education. She has a knack for finding
a good deal.

In 1987, with two daughters under the age of two, Nisa'a developed an interest in upholstery. Stumbling on an old stylish couch that,
if reupholstered, would look great in their home, she started down a
path that would evolve into stripping, pounding, and entrepreneurial
risk-taking. Although she and her husband lived comfortably with
their two daughters in a Park Hill home—his salary as a flight atten-

dant covered their living expenses and paid child support for his three sons from a previous marriage—little was left for extras. Nisa'a knew if she wanted that couch to be reupholstered, she needed to do it herself.

Attending EGOS to Learn Upholstery

Nisa'a decided to go to upholstery school. "I called the Denver School of Upholstery and was told the cost was $3,000. That was out of my budget. Someone told me about Emily Griffith. I called. They said if I was a Denver resident the cost was $16 for one day a week from 9:00 to 3:30. That was right up my alley," Nisa'a states in a pleasing, deep voice.

In 1987, Nisa'a enrolled in the Opportunity School program. Her husband arranged his schedule to be home with the children when she trekked downtown. Seriously focused on learning the skill, Nisa'a hung on the shirttails of instructor Don Kellnhofer. Like a sponge, she soaked up every trick of the trade. "I truly wanted to learn the craft...Don knew that I really wanted to learn." Students in upholstery worked on their own projects, some with the goal of going into business, others to refurbish furniture for their homes. Nisa'a was so focused on learning all aspects of the trade, her peers jokingly labeled her "teacher's pet." Attending class from 1987 to 1989, Nisa'a exited the program with skills to move to the next step.

The next chapter included practice, practice, practice. In an old, beat-up orange Volkswagen van, she and her two little girls scouted neighborhood alleys for discarded quality furniture. "In and out of the alleyways I would go, bringing home furniture." While the furniture may have looked ratty and unappealing, Nisa'a had learned in her upholstery program how to evaluate quality construction. If the junk-piled furniture appeared tattered but had solid construction with potential for a new life, she tossed it in the back of her van. Nisa'a, trim and of medium-build, appears shapely and well toned, perhaps the result of tossing around furniture for many years.

In her basement, she pounded new life into the furniture pieces, transforming them into works of art. Over the next months, Nisa'a rejuvenated so many pieces of furniture, her basement overflowed.

Her husband suggested they sell the furniture at a garage sale. With their home located close to heavily traveled Martin Luther King Boulevard, they put out their furniture at seven o'clock one Saturday morning. By two o'clock, it was all sold, and Nisa'a had pocketed $1,200. Her husband bubbled with excitement and said, "We have found something for you to do at home!"

Born in Colorado Springs in 1960, Nisa'a was the daughter of a Christian evangelist. Because her younger sister was born with cerebral palsy the family relocated to Denver when Nisa'a was seven so her sister could obtain specialized medical care. Her parents divorced when she was in high school.

After high school graduation, Nisa'a joined Frontier Airlines as a flight attendant. Attractive with a warm smile, cappuccino-colored skin, and outgoing personality, Nisa'a was well suited to be a service worker in the airlines. In this setting, she met and started dating Salahuddin, a flight attendant for United Airlines. She also became a Muslim. "I was always searching...Islam made sense." After dating for a year, she and Salahuddin married.

For the next four years, Nisa'a worked for the airlines and traveled extensively with her husband. Daughter Iram was born in 1985, and when second daughter, Ameera, arrived twenty-two months later, Nisa'a stopped working outside the home. With family as top priority, she chose to stay home and raise her children. When Ameera was eight months old, Nisa'a enrolled at Emily Griffith, and after two years of training and a successful practicum of reupholstering "alley" furniture, she discovered a home-based entrepreneurial endeavor that would complement her family responsibilities.

Operating a Home-Based Business

Nisa'a and her husband remodeled their garage into a workroom. At first, she continued to reupholster discarded furniture, but her business expanded to working on furniture for others. "People started bringing furniture to me. I did a dentist's office...I worked with an interior designer and also started hanging paper." Nisa'a's skill and talent grew in the areas of upholstery, design, and wallpapering—to the point that she redecorated a room in the 1992 Junior Symphony Guild Designer Home. Working with a designer, Nisa'a was featured in the May/June 1992 issue of *Colorado Homes and Lifestyles*. Soon she hired a neighbor part-time to strip furniture.

Working in upholstery from 1988 to 1993, she made good money, found satisfaction in her accomplishments, and successfully interwove her family and business responsibilities. During this same time, between 1989 and 1995, Nisa'a and her husband became foster parents, providing loving shelter and support to nine children. In 1992, the family moved to their current home—a solidly built, two-story, brick "Denver square," built in 1906, and located north of City Park.

In 1993, Nisa'a eased out of upholstery to focus on the "fix and flip" business she and her husband had entered in 1989. With a keen eye for good deals, they found undervalued property, purchased it, secured government assistance to fix it up, and resold it for a profit. Nisa'a again used her business sense, her penchant for hard work, and her own hands to generate money. She also focused on fixing up her home.

In the fix and flip business, Nisa'a discovered how beneficial having her own real estate license would be and knew it could increase the couple's profits. In 1998, she returned to her favorite school to pursue this training.

Returning to EGOS

In 1987, Nisa'a chose Opportunity School's upholstery program because of its reasonable tuition. In 1998, she returned to the school to study real estate because of its quality education. About her upholstery education, she said, "At the time, the reasonable tuition got me in the door. The high-quality education sold me and kept me coming back." The quality factor had beckoned her back to the school a second time.

Of course, the reasonable tuition didn't hurt. Nisa'a discovered real estate training at a private school was more than $2,000 while the same education at Opportunity School was $724. Both prepared students to pass the state licensure exam. "I trusted Emily…If you are going there to learn—whatever it may be—the information is there for you…My experience was always positive."

The real estate course proved challenging. Nisa'a plowed through the difficult legal jargon associated with the business. Although she was more knowledgeable than most as a result of her previous work, some areas were a stretch for her. Her supportive teacher, Fred Albi, said, "It will come. Real estate is like pieces of a puzzle." And for Nisa'a, it did begin to fall into place.

With less than a week remaining in the course, Nisa'a contracted bronchitis and missed the last crucial days when major reviews were conducted in preparation for the state test. Albi warned her that passing the state test would be difficult without those final days of class cramming. Motivated and disciplined, Nisa'a studied for two weeks solid, paid $150 for the test, and faced the exam head-on. She wound up passing the Colorado law portion, the most difficult aspect, but failed the practical portion by only three points. She returned a week later to retake the practical portion and passed with ease.

With license in hand, Nisa'a remained involved in the fix and flip business and also chose to try her luck at sales. She found employment at the Keller Williams central real estate office.

Finding Success in Real Estate

The first year of self-employment is lean and uphill in any business, but particularly in real estate. But she lived through it, securing her first listing and lining up business through "floor calls," responding to phone and walk-in inquiries in the real estate office. Nisa'a recalls with laughter her first customer, LeRoy, whom she assisted with a property purchase. "He was a short-statured man, wore a big cowboy hat, loved cussing, and loved being a cowboy. He was so nice. It was my first contract, and he was so patient. It took me four hours to write it…Then after that, it was repetition, and business starts to come your way." Nisa'a had written a goal of making $25,000 in her first year and was pleasantly surprised to earn $57,000.

Denver's real estate market picked up and so did Nisa'a's business. "In 2000, I could do no wrong…I remember 10:30 at night in front of K-Mart with a flashlight filling out contracts. Business was madness…The market was so crazy, in the streets all day going from one situation to another. Real estate doesn't have hours. You have to do things according to deadline. I was always running. I would leave at 7:30 in the morning and be in the car until 10:00 at night." Her long hours paid off, for her salary that year was in the six figures, an amount that again shocked her.

Nisa'a maintains a home office. She successfully transitions from career to home responsibilities with ease, like the transmission of a luxury car shifting gears with seamless motion. "Everything I have ever done has been having access to my family and them having access to me. That has been a driving force, to work out of my home." And it is easy to understand why Nisa'a wants to stay close to her comfortable home. With hardwood floors, leaded glass windows, and carved oak woodwork, the dwelling radiates an immediate sense of inviting, nostalgic comfort, a feeling of returning to grandmother's house.

Throughout her life Nisa'a has been able to recognize an underrated treasure, seize it, and spin it into a profit. She has done the same with her education at Emily Griffith Opportunity School. While some perceive the school a place for the down-and- out, Nisa'a discovered it as one of Denver's best-kept secrets. "The knowledge is there if you want to get it…Opportunity is the place to go to get fed. I give a lot of gratitude to those that help you along in life, and Emily is one of those places."

***

Author's Note: *Interviewing Nisa'a at her comfortable home was a pleasure. Her decorating talents sparkled throughout.*

DON WINFREY
Homeless Person, HVAC Technician

"Jerry Gates, the instructor, is great. Jerry would walk me through things and explain things. If I had a problem, I could tell Jerry, and he worked with me."

Living on the streets has its ups and downs. Don Winfrey knows. For close to three years, the Fox Street Bridge over the Platte River in Denver provided the only roof over his head. He struggled with a mental illness as distracting as a rattlesnake in the passenger seat of a car. Yet he ignored it. Delusional, he deemed the rest of the world crazy.

Don now belongs to the corps of the employed, making close to $36,000 annually. He lives in an apartment complex with a swimming pool and enjoys his recaptured self-respect and dignity. But his path back to the mainstream has involved many twists and turns. Emily Griffith Opportunity School embraced Don at an important junction, helping enable his remarkable turnaround.

Early Life Challenges

Don's life mirrors a car navigating through a construction zone. It has moved at a normal speed, slowed down for patches of gritty gravel, and even come to a complete stop with its engine idling. Like a vehicle traveling to its destination, however, Don has kept going.

Born in 1957 in Denver, Don moved at a young age with his father and three siblings to a small farm near La Junta, Colorado. His mother deserted the family when Don was young, and his memories of her are sketchy. The family scratched out a marginal existence from his war veteran father's disability check and their meager income from the farm.

"I lived on the farm until I was sixteen. Then I moved around a lot," says Don, taking a long drag on a cigarette. He flicks ashes into a cream-colored stoneware cereal bowl. His intense brown eyes, deep set in the sockets, concentrate. His demeanor is cautiously friendly. His long, brown hair is pulled into a pony tail.

Sitting in his small, dark apartment, Don is surrounded by walls adorned with religious pictures. An aquarium, the focal point of his living room, belches bubbles of water as its goldfish dance about gracefully. While his dwelling is not paradise, it affords a measure of comfort that is a far cry from his life on the streets.

Don's adult life began like that of many young men in their twenties. While in the Job Corps, he obtained his GED and became an apprentice in a union carpentry program. Over the next few years, he studied welding at Otero Junior College in La Junta, discovered his natural mechanical talent, and used his hands in a variety of jobs to earn his daily bread. His most promising position, a hostler's helper on the railroad, went belly-up in the recession of 1981. "When Ronald Reagan became president, I was laid off, never to return to the railroad," explains Don in a monotone voice as he chain- smokes. He shares his history in a run-on style, seldom pausing between sentences.

A Ruthless Monster Jumps on His Back

Life would begin to spiral downward at this time. Over the next few years, Don seesawed between Denver and Colorado Springs, living with his sisters, becoming a Christian, and ricocheting between jobs. Most work tapped his natural mechanical ability. At this same time, a ruthless monster had jumped on his back. Starting as a small inconvenience, the ogre grew to where Don could no longer carry it and balance a normal life. The fiend took over.

"My mental illness started to get the better of me. At that point, I could no longer work. I was probably delusional. I had some funny ideas about what was going on around me. I had a back injury, and it was getting the better of me, too. I ended up on the street. I stayed with relatives for a while, and because of my mental illness, I suppose I was scaring them. I didn't want to be around people at the time."

Short on conveniences, long on independence, street life seemed like being on a permanent camping trip. His "housemates" under the bridge included three guys struggling with drugs and alcohol. The sounds, smells, and tastes of the city enveloped them: the steady hum of overhead traffic, its odors of gaseous fumes, and the flavors and fragrances of hot soups served in charitable relief kitchens. In spite of their problems, he and his street friends looked out for each other. "There were days it got well below zero. I stayed out. I didn't like the shelters. I had a bunch of blankets. Another guy would come over and start a fire early in the morning, and we would get up and have coffee, usually instant. We would stand around the fire all morning. I did go to a few soup kitchens and got a pretty decent meal. There were places where I could shower, and I could pay for clean clothes as they were needed or I could wash them."

Don also remembers the generosity of the informal patrol—police and community volunteers—watching out for street dwellers.

"There were people keeping an eye on us. Occasionally, the police would come by, count heads, talk to us. They wouldn't harass us. Periodically, people would come down from Step 13 and the Stout Street Clinic. I remember walking by an officer in a police car. He stops me. I think, 'Oh no, I'm in trouble.' I was pretty shaggy. I had let my beard grow, and I had long hair. He said, 'Here, take this.' He gave me summer sausage and a big hunk of cheese. He said, 'Somebody gave this to me for Christmas. I'm not supposed to take it.'"

In spite of his itinerant conditions, Don held jobs during this time. His Social Security statement reflected earnings during every quarter of this period. "I got some tax money back. As my back and mental illness allowed, I periodically worked in temporaries, manual work, production work in small factories, in landscaping, and other businesses that paid cash." He used the money for cigarettes and food.

Feeling vulnerable carrying large sums of money on the street, Don worked out a deal with his sister to hide his tax refund in the sugar bowl on her kitchen table. When he needed cash, he went to her home and raided that piece of china. After several months, Don expected the money to run out. But it never did. Eyes filmed over with tears, Don says, "She is a Christian, she believes in tithing, helping the poor, and helping her family. All I can say is that the sugar bowl never went empty."

His sister's kindness notwithstanding, Don continued to live on the streets. "Basically, I kind of lived out there and wandered around. I was getting worse. There was some denial going on, and I thought the problem was with the world and not me. I was just fine."

However, Don Winfrey wanted self-respect. He longed for dignity. He wanted what most take for granted: a roof over his head, a steady job, and challenges that would bring satisfaction. In order to achieve that, he needed to face the fact he had a mental illness, and it was strangling his very being.

Don Winfrey

A Wake-up Call That Saved His Life

In October 1992, Don got the wake-up call he needed. Thin and ragged, his six-foot body had plummeted from 200 to 150 pounds. His mental state had deteriorated even further. Don recognized another winter on the street could be his last. In facing the prospect of death, he cried out for help.

Support from the Stout Street Clinic, an urban Denver facility that provides physical, mental, and dental services to low-income clients, saved his life. "Someone from there came by and talked to us. I think at that time my illness was really visible. You could tell there was something wrong. They told us if we would come in and fill out the paperwork, they would help us get a check. This was in the fall, and it was starting to get cold. So I went down there and ended up on Social Security disability with about $600 per month. Back then, that was quite a lot of money." Between the time of surrender at the clinic and the arrival of his first check, Don accessed funds for the needy, lodged in a downtown hotel, cleaned up, and started down the long, laborious road to recovery.

Uneasiness, hard work, and perseverance paved his winding path to restored health. He saw a psychiatrist through the Mental Health Corporation of Denver, and a diagnosis of schizophrenia enabled him to understand his aversion to people and inability to set priorities. He learned that people with this condition tend to be spacey and have difficulty filtering information. For schizophrenics, too much input at once is overwhelming. For example, a schizophrenic changing a baby's diaper and simultaneously hearing the buzzer of a dryer has difficulty filtering out the appliance to complete the task of changing the infant.

Slowly his condition made more sense to Don. "They measured my brain waves at the University of Colorado Health Sciences Center. After the diagnosis, they told me the classical symptoms. For the first time in my life, I started dealing with the idea, 'No, it's not the world going nuts around me.' Up to that point, I was in denial. Until you recognize you have a problem, you are not going to recover." The

189

diagnosis enabled Don to receive medicine to increase his functioning. This daily dosage now keeps him precariously balanced.

Job Training at EGOS

Don progressed to eligibility for vocational rehabilitation. Over the next two years, he worked for a warehouse—picking up donations—and steadily demonstrated improvement, eventually becoming crew supervisor. His notable progress ushered Don to a program aimed at transitioning him off Social Security and back to work. As a result, he qualified for job training.

He chose to study heating, ventilation, and air conditioning (HVAC) at Emily Griffith Opportunity School. In spite of the school's reputation for a warm, welcoming environment, Don was terrified. The academics didn't concern him, for his community college grades had been impressive. He worried about the social setting.

"I was scared to death and wanted to go back home," Don says of his first experiences at the school. "Schizophrenics are not social animals. We get in a crowd of people, and we get very self-conscious and nervous. We get into something new and we become very self-conscious."

The friendly atmosphere at the school helped Don adjust. "Jerry Gates, the instructor, is great. Jerry would walk me through things and explain things. If I had a problem, I could tell Jerry, and he worked with me. It took Jerry a while to get me calmed down. He's got a very quiet demeanor, really a kind person, also witty. It took me time to develop rapport. I don't like to share my situation with too many people, at least in the beginning. It's like wearing a sign on my forehead that says, Caution: Schizophrenic."

With Emily Griffith's support, Don moved forward. He worked four hours each night and attended classes during the day. In 1997, he graduated with certification in refrigeration. His schooling prepared him for work on residential property.

Don Winfrey

Advancing in His Field and Reclaiming His Life

Transportation limitations and a 1995 DWAI (driving while abilities are impaired) limited Don's ability to find HVAC residential work. Under the gun from Social Security to find employment, he settled for a janitorial job in state government. This job, neither lucrative nor challenging, sustained him for two years.

Eventually, a colleague recognized Don's ability and encouraged him to pursue an HVAC opening at the University of Colorado Health Sciences Center. He applied, came out at the top of the heap on their ranking system, and transferred to this new position. "I was ranked number one. I knew I had the qualifications to do this," says Don proudly.

Besides a hefty pay raise and increased responsibilities, his new job brought a bonus only schizophrenics would appreciate. He worked nights. "Pretty much I'm there alone. I like that. The buildings are totally quiet…So it's perfect for me."

When asked if he enjoys his work, Don lights up and says, "Oh it's lots of fun. Most of the time, it's quiet. We may have two hundred calls on the pager I have to address that aren't critical and are easily solved. But maybe that one in two hundred is a serious situation. I need to respond to that correctly."

And Emily Griffith Opportunity School gave him the technical skills as well as the much-needed encouragement to do his job.

Step by step, Don has reclaimed his life and improved his living conditions. After leaving the streets and the temporary downtown hotel, he was in a shared living arrangement for eleven years. He now resides in a one-bedroom apartment on Colorado Boulevard, two blocks from work.

At long last, Don is again rolling along on smooth pavement. Employed by the State of Colorado, he enjoys a full benefits package with health insurance, retirement, and cost-of-living increases. Since transferring to the HVAC job, Don has seen his salary increase almost 20 percent.

With his life more stable now, Don also remembers his textured time as a homeless person. "Sometimes I sit back and miss the freedoms I had on the street, not having to be anywhere. But I would much rather be here, having to do the work every day, living in a nice place with a swimming pool, weight room, sauna."

For Don Winfrey, life is finally good.

⚜

Author's Note: *I interviewed Don at his apartment on a winter afternoon as he sandwiched me in between his night shift work and sleep. With Don's permission, my husband accompanied me. After we left, my husband commented on Don's intelligence and his kindness. I found Don incredibly honest, open, and courageous. Since the interview, he has been promoted to a day position at UCHSC.*

KATHLEEN EGGART
Abuse Survivor, Nurse

"The nursing program gave me self-confidence. When you finish something like that, it makes you believe that you can do what you put your mind to. It gives you a strength you didn't have before."

With less than two weeks remaining in the practical nurse program at Emily Griffith Opportunity School, Kathleen Eggart feared the hard work she'd put into the 1991–1992 school year would be lost. Her arm had been severely fractured by the man she was living with, and Kathleen was physically unable to complete her remaining clinical hours. The stringent program requirements allowed little flexibility. "The instructors could either be your worst nightmare or the most wonderful people in the world," says

Kathleen, with a warm, yet serious smile. "They could be hard on you, and they had to be. The rules were the rules. If you didn't make the grade, you didn't get a second chance." Fully aware of the unyielding attendance rules, she expected to be expelled from the program.

Kathleen, who was twenty-nine at the time, had been in a relationship with this man since high school. He was also the father of her son, Nathan. In the beginning, Kathleen's boyfriend heaped emotional abuse on her. Eventually, the abuse escalated to the physical level. "As I was going through the program, things got progressively worse in our relationship, and he started a fight one night and was going to take my car. I knew if he took my car, he wouldn't bring it back and I wouldn't get to school...He picked me up and threw me in the yard and I landed with my hand behind my back and broke my left arm in three places," Kathleen states.

From the safe distance of years, she recounts her harrowing story in the modest Arvada ranch home she shares with her mother and son. The aroma of freshly brewed coffee permeates the kitchen. Her large, strong hands rest on an oilcloth covering the table that faces a north window. Several plants, including an African violet with one lone purple blossom, sit on the table and windowsill, sucking up precious sunlight.

Kathleen shares her life events of the past sixteen years in a comfortable way, expressing a wide range of emotions. With a friendly demeanor, the full-figured woman laughs easily, exposing her straight, white teeth. Her thick, long, brown hair is pulled back and fastened with a barrette.

Studying Nursing, Enduring a Destructive Relationship

Kathleen's journey to a better life started at Emily Griffith in 1989, when she enrolled in the prerequisite courses for the licensed practical nurse (LPN) program. A graduate of Arvada West High School, she had worked entry-level jobs. "I didn't know anything. I had no training...I knew if we were going to survive...there was gonna have to be a career of some kind with a little bit of money."

Like many who attend Opportunity School, Kathleen found support through Social Services. Thanks to this agency's funding, she enrolled at Emily Griffith to pursue nursing.

"I liked people," she explains. "Social Services decided to offer me the practical nurse program because I was good with my hands. I had a lot of eye-hand coordination." She gestures with fingers that sport several silver rings. The rings complement the multiple silver earrings in her ears and the silver chains around her neck.

In the fall of 1991, Kathleen enrolled in the rigorous full-time nursing program. "It was hard. If you don't make the grade, you don't make it. The class work and the clinicals are very stressful. Your instructors watch your every move."

Although they were demanding, Kathleen's instructors—Ruby Wang, Bev Karika, and Kathy Scheich—were also her role models. She now realizes their tough standards and thorough curriculum produced outstanding nurses. "You learn early in the course you're dealing with lives. You have to be sure. I remember one time we were doing blood pressures, and I said, 'I think it is 140 over 80.' Bev said, 'You can't think it's that, you have to know what it is. You have to be sure.' So I took it again and again and again until I was sure.'"

Balancing parenting, school, and a toxic relationship, Kathleen often found the simplest tasks stressful. "Everything is a big worry...one thing compounding another...When you are already worried about school, then you have to worry about where to park, that seems like a big problem." Many of her fellow classmates—also juggling the stressful demands of life, family, school, and work—dropped out of the program. According to Kathleen, of the original forty students who enrolled, only twelve to fifteen graduated.

Kathleen did not give up. She persevered and continued to struggle with the destructive relationship at home that was tearing her down and interfering with her ability to fulfill her dream of finishing school.

"There was a lot of drinking, a lot of alcohol," she explains. Kathleen's partner began to feel threatened by her success. "He saw I was going to finish the program and do better...He knew I would be making more than he would, and he said that several times. I guess he was insecure."

Often women suffering in domestic violence lose hope. Kathleen did not. "I just kept going every day, and I just kept at it. This wasn't something I wasn't going to finish...My family helped me a lot. I didn't want to disappoint them," Kathleen says.

She persevered—that is, until that fateful night when her boyfriend shattered her arm. "I had less than two weeks left, all clinical days, no more classroom. We had taken all our tests. I had passed everything. We just *had* to be there," Kathleen explains. But with her injury, it seemed impossible to claim that diploma she had worked so hard to attain. Thankfully, her teachers proved to be more understanding than Kathleen had envisioned. She approached them with her plaster-encased arm as evidence, explained her home situation, and asked for their support. They devised a plan for her to finish the program.

Capturing the LPN Certificate, Leaving Town, Finding Work

When she was able, Kathleen completed the required clinical hours to qualify for her LPN certificate. With the hard-won nursing certification under her belt, Kathleen left town with Nathan, leaving behind her son's father. Hoping to begin a new chapter in their lives, they headed to Palisade, Colorado, where Kathleen's father lived. She passed her state boards and landed a job in a long-term care facility close to her dad's home.

Still, this was not the direction she had envisioned for her career. While in nurses' training, Kathleen swore she would never work in nursing homes. However, her unreliable car dictated she take a job within walking distance of her father's house. The nearby long-term care facility provided the only alternative.

Ironically, for all her dread and anticipation, Kathleen's nursing home experience unfolded positively. Her green eyes dance as she talks about her work. "I found my niche in long-term care. Through the course of that job, it turned into something I liked." Kathleen says, "I love the residents. I love taking care of them…I figure, good Lord, they have been around ninety years, and they deserve the best you can give them. These people worked so many years. They deserve to have somebody take good care of them."

In this most unlikely place, Kathleen's professional life soared. At the same time, her son's father claimed he had changed and had stopped drinking. He wanted to be with Kathleen and Nathan. Ever trusting, Kathleen believed him. She decided to give their relationship another chance. He moved to Grand Junction, and they married in 1993.

Other changes followed. "I went to work at the long-term care facility that was attached to the VA Medical Center, and it was the best place to work." While her career thrived, her personal life deteriorated once more. Her husband reverted to his old ways and seldom worked. "It would build up. He would drink. He would be home with Nathan…would be drunk in the chair and would have no idea where Nathan was. The drinking kept getting worse. The verbal abuse kept getting worse," Kathleen explains remorsefully.

Finding Confidence and Strength

Kathleen realized she had made a terrible mistake in marrying this man. Christmas Day of 1994 proved to be the clincher. "He was real nasty that day. He grabbed Nathan…I said, 'That's enough.' When he passed out, Nathan and I left. I just got tired of feeling that way. I knew I was doing wrong. It was a wrong relationship. Just knowing he could make me feel terrible, run me down like I was worth nothing…I had to quit."

Kathleen's steady accumulation of accomplishments armed her with the fortitude she needed to move forward. "I had had enough. I probably wouldn't have had the strength…the self-confidence to stay away. The nursing program gave me self-confidence. When you finish something like that, it makes you believe you can do what you put your mind to. It gives you a strength you didn't have before." After eighteen months of marriage, Kathleen divorced. This time, reinforced by her school and career successes, she mustered the strength to leave permanently and fashion a life on her own.

"The education at Emily Griffith Opportunity School made me believe that I could stand up for myself. I could stand my ground. It gave me confidence in my own decisions."

In 1996, fortified with courage and clarity, Kathleen returned to Denver with Nathan. She has not reconnected with her former husband, although her son remains in contact with his father.

Rebounding to a New, Satisfying Life

For many, moving to a new community without a job is as terrifying and inconceivable as jumping from a plane without a parachute. Yet Kathleen always found abundant employment opportunities in the health care field when she needed them. In Denver, she easily secured a position in long-term care.

Kathleen happily discovered her training at Opportunity School opened doors. "I never had trouble getting jobs. Any job I have applied for, I have gotten. One of the places hired me because they knew Emily Griffith trained their nurses well." In hindsight, she realized the benefits of EGOS's tough standards. Their outstanding nursing graduates would be in demand in the industry.

More than a decade after her EGOS training, as Kathleen carries out her nursing responsibilities, she senses her strict teachers looking over her shoulder. "I still think when I'm on the job, 'Okay, if Ruby saw me doing this, what would she think? Or if Bev was standing there watching me, what would she say?' One day, I got locked in the Alzheimer's unit and I thought, 'What would they say?' Even ten years later, I still think that. I probably always will. I respect those teachers so much I still want to please them. I want them to be proud of me."

In nursing, Kathleen has found more than abundant employment opportunities. She has found her passion. "I love nursing. I have been working in the Alzheimer's unit, and I just love it. It is very rewarding."

Kathleen and Nathan, who is now a high school graduate and making his own way in the world, moved out of the grips of an abusive relationship because of the confidence Kathleen gleaned from nurses' training and her subsequent achievements in her career. Years later, that unfortunate relationship remains a distant, yet ugly, reminder of her rocky past. Kathleen's scars have healed because of her courage to take her life into her own hands and because of the rewarding career she has found in nursing. Emily Griffith Opportunity School equipped her with the confidence and skills she needed to achieve this noteworthy success.

***

Author's Note: *Because of a shoulder injury, Kathleen Eggart was forced to leave her beloved work in long-term care. She now works in a gastroenterology practice and enjoys a schedule that includes weekend and holiday breaks.*

*The doors to opportunity and achievement are always open at
Emily Griffith Opportunity School.*

Bibliography

"A Century of Colorado Census," compiled by Suzanne Schultze. Revised 1977 with microfilm collection by Robert Markham, Michener Library, University of Northern Colorado, Greeley.

"Adult School Fees Illegal, Board Hears." *Denver Post,* July 14, 1957.

"Aircraft Mechanics Training Moved to Stapleton Site." *Denver Post,* January 24, 1968.

"Awards Scheduled in WINs Program." *Denver Post,* May 27, 1971.

Barrett, William E. "Emily Griffith—Gift of Sod Hut." *Rocky Mountain News,* May 20, 1962.

"Bill Drafted to Create System of Colorado Vocational Colleges." *Denver Post,* February 12, 1967.

Bingham, Janet. "Opportunity School Faces Pressure to Charge Tuition." *Denver Post,* August 23, 1987.

Bishop, Ann. "Vietnam Refugees Helped on Way to U.S. Citizenship." *Denver Post,* March 29, 1978.

Bluemel, Elinor. *Emily Griffith and the Opportunity School of Denver.* Denver: privately printed, 1954.

———. *The Golden Opportunity: The Story of the Unique Emily Griffith Opportunity School of Denver.* Boulder: Johnson Publishing Company, 1965.

———. *The Opportunity School and Emily Griffith Its Founder.* Denver: Green Mountain Press, 1970.

Chronis, Peter G. "Founder Saw Special School Needed for Adult Education." *Denver Post,* July 20, 1997.

Clearfield, Elaine Abrams. *Our Colorado Immortals in Stained Glass.* Library of Congress Catalog Publication, 1986.

Cox, Jack. "Colorado's Unsolved Mysteries Caiman Is Odd But Other Tales Even More Curious." *Denver Post,* September 1, 1998.

"Denver's True Value." *Denver Post,* October 9, 1987.

Doel, Marcie. "ADC Moms Inspired by Homemaker Class." *Denver Post,* January 21, 1974.

"Educator Emily Griffith, Virginia Blue Win Window Vote." *Rocky Mountain News,* February 20, 1975.

"8,400 B.A. min [Minimum] in Denver." *Colorado Teacher,* January 1970.

"Emily Griffith to Open New Training Shops." *Denver Post,* October 16, 1955.

"Emily Griffith Tuition Plan Opposed." *Denver Post,* October 10, 1976.

Ewegen, Bob. "3 Windows Dedicated in State Senate." *Denver Post,* January 7, 1976.

"Executive Order: Proclamation Emily Griffith Stained Glass Window Rededication Day, February 10, 1986," State of Colorado, January 23, 1986, Richard D. Lamm, Governor

Faulkner, Debra. *Touching Tomorrow: The Emily Griffith Story.* Palmer Lake, Colo.: Filter Press, 2005.

Flanagan, Mike. "Emily Griffith Educator." *Denver Post Magazine,* March 23, 1986.

Flynn, Kevin. "14 Celebrate Welfare Freedom." *Rocky Mountain News,* November 14, 1987.

———. "17 Individuals, Organizations Picked for Millennium Award." *Rocky Mountain News,* June 21, 1999.

"Front Range Airport Finds Room for Student Mechanics." *Denver Business Journal,* September 19–25, 2003.

Gaskie, Jack. "Adult Education Takes 5 Percent of School Budget." *Rocky Mountain News,* September 20, 1957.

———. "Legislators Explore Opportunity School." *Rocky Mountain News,* July 14, 1962.

"Griffith to Build New Mechanic Shop." *Southeast Sentinel,* December 21, 1977.

Halaas, David Fridtjob. "Emily Griffith: 'Let Me Tell You of a Hope.'" *Colorado History Now,* June 1999.

Huffman, Yale. *The Life and Death of Emily Griffith.* Denver: privately printed, 1989.

———. "Prairie Pluck: The Mission of Emily Griffith." *Sunday World-Herald of the Midlands,* February 21, 1988.

Jain, Bob. "Aviation Training Addition Dedicated by Emily Griffith." *Denver Post,* May 13, 1977.

Lee, Betty Jean. "Desire to Learn Links Poor and Well-to-Do." *Denver Post,* March 23, 1986.

Margolin, Morton L. "Electronics Firm to Locate in Denver." *Rocky Mountain News,* March 20, 1970.

Marranzino, Pasquale. "Mercy Motive in Killing of Emily Griffith." *Rocky Mountain News,* June 20, 1947.

McCoy, Joan. "Opportunity's There for Fun in the Kitchen." *Rocky Mountain News,* February 16, 1973.

Meadow, James B. "Secrets of State Colorado History Has Its Share of Unfinished Business." *Rocky Mountain News,* June 21, 1999.

Nebraska State Census of 1885, Custer County, Arnold Precinct.

"Opportunity School Brings City Firms." *Denver Post,* July 14, 1957.

"Opportunity School Has Millionth Student." *Denver Post,* February 15, 1972.

"Opportunity School to Cost Denver Residents Tuition Fees." *Denver Herald Dispatch,* September 2, 1993.

"Plan Makes WINners of Welfare Recipients." *Denver Post,* May 28, 1969.

Plumb, Francis. "If She Had Married." *Rocky Mountain News,* June 18, 1954.

Rees, Tom. "Denver Schools Ordered to Adopt Court Plan to End All Segregation." *Rocky Mountain News*, April 18, 1974.

Romano, Michael. "Emily Griffith's Violent Death Followed Life of Service." *Sunday Magazine, Rocky Mountain News,* February 18, 1990.

"School Gets Jets." *Denver Post,* March 1, 1970.

"Seminar Set for Women in Business." *Denver Post,* January 20, 1974.

Stoenner, Herb. "Help Is There for Pregnant Teens Who Want." *Denver Post,* March 3, 1976.

U.S. Bureau of the Census. "Characteristics of the Population, Part 7, Colorado, 1970." Issued by the U.S. Department of Commerce, Washington, D.C., 1973.

U.S. Federal Census, State of Ohio, Hamilton County, 1870.

Vogt, Katherine. "School Haven for Adults: Emily Griffith Targets Reading." *Denver Post,* May 3, 1996.

Weber, Brian. "Teacher Knew about Compassion." *Rocky Mountain News,* September 7, 1999.

Woodfin, Max. "Oldest Graduate Takes All in Stride." *Rocky Mountain News,* June 6, 1976.

————. "Opportunity School Tuition Eyed." *Rocky Mountain News,* August 12, 1976.

Sources from Emily Griffith Opportunity School

Annual Descriptive Reports of the Emily Griffith Opportunity School, 1942–1943 to 1978–1979.

Articles from *The Welton Street Journal,* quarterly newsletter of the Emily Griffith Opportunity School, 1975–2001.

Budget and program data from Dee Wood, comptroller, Emily Griffith Opportunity School.

Discussion with Estelle Matus, retired instructional dean of English as a Second Language, Emily Griffith Opportunity School, February 2004.

Discussion with Marilyn Bowlds, executive director of the Emily Griffith Foundation, January 2005.

Emily Griffith Foundation Annual Report, 2001.

Emily Griffith Opportunity School catalogs, 1987–2005.

Enrollment data from Marilyn Miller, data specialist, Technology Support Center, Emily Griffith Opportunity School.

50th Year, 1916–1966, Denver Public Schools, Emily Griffith Opportunity School, Adult, Vocational, and Technical Education, Denver, Colorado 80204.

Index

Index

Index

Acknowledgments

Thank you to

Those who willingly shared their stories and inspiration with me. Because of space limitations, these stories could not be included: Donna Fedelina Madrid Aragon, John Bowman, Jeannine Glau, Rebecca Gonzales, Ming Her, Cheri Issel, Mark Long, Michael Hodapp, Dave Hoffman, Felipe Perez, and Shawn Sherwood.

The Emily Griffith Foundation for its tremendous support, with special thanks to Marilyn Bowlds whose encouragement and enthusiasm sustained me every step of the way, and to Donna House, who served as my ever-present 'agent,' occasional photographer, and ongoing promoter.

Mary Saracino, writing coach, mentor, cheerleader, and most of all, friend.

Janet Metzenbaum, Ellen Wynn, Marsha Celesta, and Loretta Ukulele for their help with that ever-challenging rascal: my computer.

Mayor John W. Hickenlooper, Dr. Thomas Noel, and Dick Kreck for carving time out of their busy schedules to write the foreword and back cover comments, respectively.

Emily Griffith Opportunity School staff who granted permission for use of historic photos and gave me free rein to explore the school archives as well as offered suggestions for subjects to interview, provided valuable school information, and gave supportive feedback on sections they read. Special thanks to Marilyn Miller for all her help.

The many who read stories in this book and offered helpful suggestions. They include fellow aspiring writers in Lighthouse writing workshops, as well as friends, colleagues, and family members.

Jody Berman and Sharon Popish for their editing assistance.

PJ Pierce, an accomplished Texas author who shared materials and insights, and to our mutual friend, Linda Acker, who connected us.

Ken Raak, my husband of twenty-one years, who knew more than anyone my deep love and appreciation for Emily Griffith Opportunity School and who patiently supported this writing project as a labor of love for the school. Most of all, I thank him for all he did to make this dream a reality.

About the Author

Carolyn Brink spent fifteen years as an administrator at Emily Griffith Opportunity School, serving as coordinator of Consumer and Family Studies, assistant principal, and director of Support Services. Prior to that, she served four years as a program manager at the Colorado Community College System, six years as an assistant professor at the University of Northern Colorado, and two years as a secondary teacher in Minnesota.

A native of South Dakota, she earned a doctorate of philosophy from Oklahoma State University. She retired from EGOS in 2003 and currently serves on the Board of Directors of the Emily Griffith Foundation. When not traveling, she and her husband, Ken Raak, can be found at their home in south Denver.

Additional copies of

Class Acts: Stories from Emily Griffith Opportunity School

are available at your local bookstore or online at *www.filterpressbooks.com*

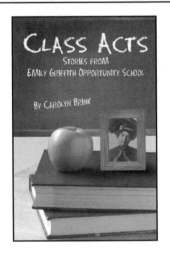

Class Acts may also be ordered from the Emily Griffith Foundation at 720.423.4722